Praise for Adventure Devos

These two not only know adventure, but they also know God's Word, clearly connecting crazy, dangerous pursuits to solid, applicable truths from Scripture. I can easily see men, women, and even youth enjoying the stories here, all while being drawn to spend more time in God's Word as a result. What God does from there, who can guess?

I certainly wish I'd had this book for all my years of youth ministry. Still, this is definitely the devotional for the "Wild at Heart" crowd.

> Rob Cook, Pastor, Speaker, Author of *Regener8*, and Youth Pastor to Street Smart Teens. Speaker website: www.robcookunderground.com

I've slept on narrow ledges above raging rivers and stood waist deep in snowmelt streams with Eric and I can honestly say, he is the real deal when it comes to adventure. It may not be Everest, but what he's up to is just as crazy, and a whole lot closer to home.

> Virginia "V" Beineke, at 20 yrs old, the youngest participant to ever be invited to—and complete—what's been called one of the toughest endurance races ever, the 2018 Alaskaman Extreme Triathlon

This book perfectly captures the types of adventures open to just about anyone, anywhere, these days. Not only are you "dared" to take action on what you read and learn with easy, everyday choices, but you can also take on most of the adventures listed too, without having to travel to the other side of the world.

> Curtis Kincaid, ultra-marathoner, 2018 Pikes Peak Ascent participant, and co-leader, Catalyst Hiking Ministry, Woodmen Valley Chapel, Colorado Springs, Colorado

Men love risk, and every guy loves a challenge. The insights offered here are going to challenge you to be a better leader, team member, or friend. As long as you're going to take a risk and go skydiving, why not let this book motivate and encourage you to take the risk to love your wife more or be a better boss, too.

> Ralph Miller, former SWAT team member, Orange County Sheriff's office, Orlando, Florida, and FBI Organized Crime/Terrorism Task Force member

These two adventure fanatics took every risky experience that didn't kill them and turned them into illustrations of God's wisdom for everyday living, backed up by Scripture. Amazing. A great devotional read for any man.

> Colonel Douglas Hinkley, U.S. Army Brigade Commander and former Commander in Iraq, tasked with Distinguished Visitor and Congressional Protection Services during Operation Iraqi Freedom

Ladies, want a devotional that the men in your life will actually get excited about? You're looking at it. *Adventure Devos* will challenge any man to be a better father or husband in no time, no doubt about it.

Just read a few of the book's "Dares" and see for yourself how easily this devotional will get anyone into applying God's Word.

> Megan Autrey, Colorado Certified Whitewater Guide Instructor, Wife and Mother

Adventure Devos

The first devotional
written exclusively for
men with a heart for
RISK AND DANGER

by

Eric Sprinkle
and
Sam Evans

Living a life
that's challenging,

**ADVENTURE
EXPER✦ENCE**

exhilarating and
eye-opening   TM

Adventure Experience Press
Colorado Springs, Colorado

Adventure Devos

ISBN: 978-1-7322694-0-8

First printing 2018

Published by Adventure Experience Press

All photos by the authors

Cover design by Robert Baddorf

Dedication

Eric

To my first love—Christine. I'm so sorry you were called home before you could see this book realized. No matter, you still totally made it happen.

To my next love, whom I've yet to meet—I look forward to the many adventures just waiting to be shared!

Sam

To my husband, Clint—who challenges me and humors me and lives this life adventure beside me.

To my precious daughters, Kaylynn, Kelly and Trinity—some of the best things in life happen to us when we are outdoors and dirty. Cheers to the adventures you're just beginning.

Table of Contents

Foreword

Sam here. If you like to hike, climb, run whitewater—or at least like to read about it—you've come to the right place. However, it would be a great injustice to put this amazing devotional in your hand without sharing with you the genesis of how it came to be.

I flew out Wednesday morning, May 17th, to attend the Colorado Christian Writer's Conference in Estes Park, Colorado. The greetings at the conference closely resembled a college freshman orientation. But instead of, "What's your major," participants asked, "What do you write?"

During one of these introductions, I pointed to the name tag on my collarbone and said, "Hi. I'm Sam, from Sleepy Eye."

But we never arrived at the "What do you write?" question, because the guy I introduced myself to pinched the fleece at his collarbone and, finding it nametag-less, said, "Hi. I'm North Face. Nice to meet you." From there, the conversation went off-roading.

"Hi. I'm North Face. Nice to meet you."

And that, friends, is the moment that Eric Sprinkle and Sam Evans became friends.

That very same day, 42 inches of snow fell in 36 hours in Estes Park. Roads closed, trapping some people in while keeping others out. The sheer amount of snow forced the clock's rotation to slow down.

Of course, the snow didn't bother me. It was gorgeous and I'm from Minnesota, "where people help people get stuck cars out of the snow for fun," adventurer extraordinaire Eric Sprinkle noted, as I came in from outside. I shrugged and smiled. With great boots comes great responsibility.

I hiked out the next morning before the sun rose on the white forest. In that stillness, I felt as if God was trudging through the snow beside me, and I felt God sifting me. Ugly corners of my heart required attention and I became God's captive audience.

When was the last time you stepped off the page of your Choose-Your-Own-Adventure life and granted God an opportunity to speak to your heart?

When was the last time you stepped off the page of your Choose-Your-Own-Adventure life?

The thrust of these devotions, then, is to make that time alone with God more accessible, more exciting, and more meaningful. And—no snowstorms required. The illustrations are crazy, the dares are real, and we hope you'll share your experiences with the other people in your life, propelling them toward their own time with God.

Not sure what this should all look like? How about this? Go through the book doing just two devotions per week. That's it. And take on the dares knowing that what you put into them is what you'll get out.

When we read God's word, life change is inevitable. When we do what it says, even more so. The people around you will notice.

Whatever your God-time looks like, it's in your hands now. So strap on your helmet, grab some climbing shoes and join us between these pages. The adventure awaits!

Acknowledgements

This book is independently published, not self-published. Nobody ever publishes a book by themselves.

The exceptional people who helped us make Adventure Devos a reality, then, are the following:

- **Line-editing:** "Hiker" Amy Zepeda (www.AmyZepeda.com)

- **Editing:** "Hiker" Debbie Hardy (www.DebbieHardy.com)

- **Formatting and typesetting:** "Woodsman" David Fessenden (www. davefessenden.com/honeycomb-house-publishing-llc/)

- **Cover Art:** "Explorer" Rob

- **Beta Readers:** "Mountain Climber" Curtis, his wife "Hiker" Connie, "Whitewater" Julie, "Forest Firefighter" and "Man's Man" Paul, "Caver" Jeff, and "Surfer" Paul

- **Also:** "Skydiver" Robert, "King of the Raft" Steven, "Sailor/ Skier" Carissa, "Ice-Fisher" Joe and "Canoer" Jamie

- **Special thanks to:** Taco Bell® (Colorado Springs, CO) and Hardee's® (Sleepy Eye, MN) for a place to lay our laptops

We are so truly thankful to our amazing heavenly Father for years of safe adventuring, and the opportunity to now share those same adventures in a way that can inspire and help open doors to God's truths for living.

Soli Deo Gloria.

Getting Sandy in the Grand Canyon

Staying pure in a sinful world
Read Ephesians 5:3-20

When traveling on a river trip in the Grand Canyon it doesn't really matter how many days you'll spend. The simple fact is that by some point, you, and everything you own, are going to be covered in sand.

It happens slowly, and there is an element of disbelief throughout, but here's how it generally works.

Day 1: That guy over there with sand in his sleeping bag? Not me. No way. I am going to be sand-free.

Day 2: Okay, somehow some sand got into my sleeping bag too, but that's over.

Day 3: Okay, sand continues to get into my sleeping bag despite my best efforts. I'll just have to live with it.

Day 4: The sand in my sleeping bag has now saturated my hair, it's in my ears, and I swear there was some grit swishing around my mouth as I drank coffee this morning.

Day 5: Okay, you know what? It's just going to be a "sand everywhere" kind of trip, but so help me, I am NOT going to allow any sand getting into my _____.

What would you put in that blank? Camera? Sensitive electronics? Coffee mug is another popular answer to that question. If everything I own is going to get sandy, where do I absolutely, positively draw the line?

Paul refers to this same issue in our lives here on earth. We are immersed in a culture that we do not belong to, but grime gets all over us, anyway. We are pilgrims traveling through a land we do not call home, and yet the sin so easily gets in and becomes part of us.

Where do you draw the line? Where do you say, "This far and no further?"

Be very careful, then, how you live—not as unwise but as wise, making the most of every opportunity...
Ephesians 5:15-16

Is it in your speech? Are there words or phrases you simply will not use, obscene or not, simply because they convey a coarseness that is the exact opposite of the purity of Christ you are striving to reflect?

Maybe it's your choice of movies. Maybe you draw the line at content ratings, or just as likely genres; ones that you will not watch, regardless of how popular they are with friends. You may or may not quote them, might laugh along at references, but will never view them. Ever.

On the Grand, I decided which items I would brutally protect by the simple questions of a) would it cause something not to work? or b) would it bring discomfort to me or others? Electronics, food, and my toothbrush all fell into this category.

Sand in my books? Okay. In my outdoor gear? Sure, fine. And even after a deep breath, I could live with it in my sleeping bag, because that's just the nature of the environment. It's a little naive to go on a trip in the Grand Canyon and not expect to get sand in your things. Thinking otherwise is either unrealistic, or requires you to pull yourself completely out of the environment.

Similarly, it's only realistic to expect we'll get spiritually dirty from our surroundings in this life. We brush against others in the Marketplace of Ideas, trudge through spiritual muck, and get smelly whenever we hang out with others that smell of this fallen world. But that's simply the cost of sharing Christ in a sinful world. Just so long as it doesn't remove our "saltiness," doesn't dull our light, there's no problem.

"You are the salt of the earth. But if the salt loses its saltiness, how can it be made salty again? It is no longer good for anything, except to be thrown out and trampled underfoot."

Matthew 5:13

The disciples' feet needed washing. Christ used it as an example of servant leadership, but also, that was just the nature of the desert environment. If you're going to reflect Christ in this world, understand that "sand" is going to get into everything. And it's going to be uncomfortable. But that doesn't mean we step out of this world, nor do we give up and let the sand take over. Not at all.

Draw the line. Choose this day what you're going to protect from the dirt and grime of this world. Stay salty. Stay bright.

And encourage your fellow travelers that they need not put up with this world's annoying "sand" getting into everything they own, either.

Dare—I'm guessing you already have "rules" in your life: a "swear jar" or limits on movies. Review them with family members, roommates, or a trusted friend. Need any updating?

Double Dare—Create an entirely new rule for staying bright. No more saying that crude or coarse word. No more watching R films alone. Anything works. Charge a $.25 - $1 fine if you do. Proceeds go towards taking kids, wife/sweetie, or good friends out for fast food.

Triple Dare—Here's your new rule: You watch a movie, then catch yourself repeating dialogue you shouldn't, or reviewing 'steamy scenes' in your head after, and it automatically goes in the "Do Not Watch" pile for one year. No matter how cool, our movies simply do not get to direct our behavior.

The Day I Almost Drowned

God saves us from tragedy
Read Matthew 14:22-33

My body slammed into the water. *Cold!* I tried to orient myself. The orange sail lay flat on the surface of the water, five feet above me, but when I finally reached it, I found myself trapped in an airless vacuum between the fabric and the water.

Has anything bad *almost* ever happened to you? I have way too many examples.

In my college years, I worked as a camp counselor during the summers. One perfect day, a co-counselor and I had some downtime, and he invited me to go sailing. There should be a Jeopardy category for "Questions Sam Should Ask First."

There should be a Jeopardy category for
"Questions Sam Should Ask First."

We were out in the middle of the lake when I casually asked, "So, how many times have you done this?"

"Oh, this is my second time. And the first time by myself." The sailboat capsize was inevitable.

Fast forward five years. My husband and I went whitewater rafting. We sat at the back of the raft. Recovering from a hard drop, a man at the front fell into the rapids. The water was deep enough that he went under. Before anyone had a chance to panic, my husband plunged his arm into the water, got a fistful of life jacket and pulled the man back into the raft.

Most of us have experienced tragedies or almost-tragedies. It is impossible to survive life unscathed. All of us have experienced brokenness. I am not referring to the time that I broke my mom's Currier and Ives butter dish (sorry, Mom). I am speaking of broken families, broken relationships, broken finances—broken moments.

19

Broken moments last longer. Time does not travel at the same speed when we are experiencing distress or anguish.

In reality, only 20 seconds or so passed from the time that the sailboat capsized, to the time that my face broke the surface and I gulped air. But, I remember the boat tipping. I remember straddling the edge and scrambling, futilely, to stay aboard. I remember the position of my body as I hit the water. The way the sun looked, filtered through a bright orange sail, from beneath the surface.

Unable to draw breath, I panicked.

My life jacket propelled me upward. The nylon sail, suctioned to the water's surface, provided no air space. Unable to draw breath, I panicked. Where was the edge? Which way should I turn? Yet, my mind cleared with a determined focus. My lungs burning, I grabbed fistfuls of the fabric, yanking and kicking my way to the sail's edge.

I remember my first breath.

I swiveled in the water and spotted the other counselor (whose name I can't even remember). "Are you okay?" we simultaneously shouted at one another with adrenaline-pitched voices.

Reassured, I let my body relax. The water felt cool on the back of my scalp as I floated like a buoy in the water.

Maybe 30 seconds had passed.

I'm sure time moved slower for the man who fell into the rapids as well. His mind had time to conjure a thousand fears. And when my husband's arm plunged beneath the surface and snatched his life jacket, the arm seemed to take much longer to reach him than it did to those of us on the raft, moving down the current in real time.

Many of you know the story of "Peter Sinks in the Sea of Galilee" a.k.a. "Jesus Walks on Water" (Matt. 14:22-33).

Here are the CliffsNotes®: disciples in a boat in the middle of the sea, pre-dawn. Jesus on shore. Blustery night. Jesus casually walked out atop the waves toward the boat. The disciples panicked.

"Take courage! It is I. Don't be afraid."

"Heh. If you're really Jesus, tell me to walk out on the water," Peter said.

"Come." He knew that Peter, like Sam Evans, was a sucker for a good dare. "I triple-dog dare you" (Sam Paraphrase Translation).

Peter crawled over the lip of the boat. Then he freaked out. He began to sink. He could have saved himself a lot of trouble—and laundry—if he'd simply panicked from within the boat, like the rest of the disciples.

"Immediately Jesus reached out his hand and caught him. 'You of little faith. Why did you doubt?' And when they climbed into the boat, the wind died down" (Matt. 14:31-32).

Now, the Bible says, "immediately," but I would wager that "immediately" didn't feel so immediate to the drowning, panicking Peter, right?

Peter *almost* drowned. It was almost a thing. But it wasn't a thing. Because Jesus was there.

They climbed into the boat, and immediately the wind died down.

My encouragement to you is that time seems to move more slowly in the midst of dark moments. You have time for a million prayers, and feel as if God is ignoring you, but that simply isn't true. God hears you. He cares for you. He sees what is happening, and he is faithful.

So, sit back, put your feet up, and trust that God is present within your rocking boat.

––––––––––

Dare—Have you ever been in a situation where you feared for your life? Recall the story. In light of today's devo, contemplate how you might have handled it differently.

Double Dare—Worried about something? Take Philippians 4:6-7 to heart and go do something to get your heart pumping. Thanking God and taking a run have all sorts of benefits that reduce worry. Did you know that getting outside in nature, just that alone, can lower stress?

Triple Dare—When's the last time you went sailing? How about white-water rafting? I'm guessing you have one or the other within a few hours of you. Been meaning to do it? Put it on the calendar today, or, why not just make it happen this weekend?

Skydiving and Choosing Wrong

Our daily wrestling match
Read Romans 7:14-25

Skydiving. You can do it almost anywhere these days, on any week-end, either tightly tethered to another person (tandem), or taking a class and jumping all alone (static-line). A few years ago, I had the privilege to try it myself. My choice? Static-line.

While relatively easy (think WWII paratroopers), the reality is that even though the airplane "pulls" your chute for you, there are still a number of things that can go wrong up there: tangled lines, a snagged chute, or a canopy that doesn't fully deploy... This was going to be the real thing.

On the morning of the jump, I spent four hours training on skydiving theory, parachute canopies, brake deployment, and safe landing proce-dures. We all jumped from four feet into pea gravel to practice the tuck and roll. Hung from a harness and pulled simulated tabs. Rehearsed our jump mantra of, "Red dot! Arch-1,000, 2-1,000, 3-1,000, 4-1,000, clear!" over and over again. At the end of class, while taping down potential snag points on our boots, two of us were called off to the side.

Uh-oh. Where did we screw up?

One of the instructors warned us that our body proportions (i.e. taller, long arms) posed a special risk that we in particular should know about.

Apparently, you should never feel "butterflies" while skydiving. This phenomenon doesn't actually occur in nature and is a by-product of amusement parks, namely anything dragging you downward faster than the normal rate at which you would fall. Roller coasters and Tower-of-Terror rides cause butterflies, but never skydiving...unless.

During your static-line jump, one of your jobs, once you've verified a good canopy above you, is to grasp your brake handles and pull down sharply, allowing you to maneuver your parachute, pulling the right or left brake to rotate that direction. It's cool, but come to find out, if you have really long arms, you can apparently pull them too hard.

Too hard? Well, just enough to cause your canopy to stall. Yes, stall. And as you are 2,500 feet above the ground, you have absolutely no reference that this is happening…except for the butterflies. "If you pull both brakes downward and start to feel butterflies in your stomach," he shared, "that means you're stalling and your canopy is slipping backwards and pulling you down." He demonstrated the concept by holding both hands, one above the other, and then showing how they flip over and one hand falls into the other.

"Please note," he told us, "you cannot cut away from a failed canopy and deploy your reserve chute if you've already fallen backwards into it." He dryly explained that the fabric would wrap itself around you as you plummeted back towards earth. Good to know.

We marched out to the waiting aircraft. It was time to jump.

And with that cautionary note, we rejoined the group, pulled on our chutes, and marched nervously out to the waiting aircraft. It was time to jump.

Quickly achieving altitude, one by one we stepped out onto the landing gear, grabbed the wing strut tightly, set our focus, and let go. Falling away into the warm afternoon sky, billows of fabric and cordage streamed up and away from us. All canopies deployed correctly, we all navigated our way to the landing area and, one after another, dropped into the loose gravel, rolling to our knees and back up to a standing position, broad smiles spread across our faces as we pulled in armloads of loose canopy fabric.

High fives were exchanged, nervous admissions of "I was so scared!" were shared by many, and at one point I wandered over to my fellow tall, long-armed jumper and asked as nonchalantly as I could, "So did you do it? That stall-your-canopy thing?"

"Yup," he answered, with a covert grin.

"Me too," I smiled back.

So, having been told of the extreme danger and potentially fatal consequences of stalling your canopy, of course the two of us just naturally had to give it a try. Seriously?!?

What is it about doing the wrong thing that naturally calls to us? Tell anyone NOT to press that button (the pretty, candy-colored button?) and they will instantly be fixated on it. Any sociologist who thinks people are inherently good at heart is missing something terribly obvious. We wrestle with choosing what's right every day of our lives.

We can hardly contain this sinful nature that compels us to do wrong. Even Paul, apostle of Christ and preeminent New Testament author, wrestled with this himself, sharing his struggles in Romans 7:15, saying, "I do not understand what I do. For what I want to do, I do not do, but what I hate I do." You can just hear the frustration.

What is it about doing the wrong thing that naturally calls to us?

Skydiving no-no's, eating too many donuts, thinking mean thoughts about others. It just never seems to end.

So what do we do? Hope that God is gracious and that we don't fall from the sky and kill our stupid selves after being clearly told "what not to do"? Reflect back on today's verses and keep reading Paul's thoughts through the very end of chapter seven, because there it is. The ultimate question in our struggle of right vs. wrong.

"What a wretched man I am! Who will rescue me from this body that is subject to death?" he pleads in verse 24. Translated as "body of death" in the ESV—this is a reference to the barbaric Roman practice of tightly tying a dead body to a living man until the diseased, rotting corpse finally causes his death. This then, is the truly ugly face of our struggle. But there is an answer, found in the very next verse as Paul clearly articulates the hope for both him and ourselves, back then, right now, and forever more, calling out, "Thanks be to God, who delivers me through Jesus Christ our Lord!" (Rom. 7:25).

Christ in me, my hope of glory, is able to keep me from stumbling (Jude 1:24). And it's not with hesitation that he offers a hand, or out of disappointment that he helps me. No, according to the author Jude, Jesus takes on this process, no kidding, "with great joy!" I love it!

"To him who is able to keep you from stumbling and to present you before his glorious presence without fault and with great joy—to the only God our Savior be glory, majesty, power and authority, through Jesus Christ our Lord, before all ages, now and forevermore" (Jude 1:24-25).

Want to blame it on the Evil One? Maybe, but I think we all too often give our enemy far more credit than he's worth. No, my old sinful heart is capable of falling for temptation all by itself, thank you.

In a world of slow drivers, yoga pants, and chocolate cake, we can still be victorious.

So always remember that there is no temptation that we cannot stand up under (1 Cor. 10:13). Christ himself wrestled with it too, and won (Heb. 4:15). We can be truly confident that he is able to keep us "until that day" (2 Tim. 1:12). Lean on Christ. Fill yourself with his Word. Ask him to strengthen you, and watch the tide start to turn.

In a world of slow drivers in the fast lane, slender women in yoga pants, and chocolate cake, we can still be truly victorious in the struggle with our sinful natures. Thanks be to God indeed.

Dare—Read today's verses in Romans out loud, with feeling. That's right. Feel free to wait until you're alone, but you're doing it right if the dog looks alarmed when you reach verse 25.

Double Dare—Memorize verses 24 and 25. Recite them to yourself (out loud, with feeling anyone?) anytime you see potential for mayhem, i.e. sex scenes on TV, stop-and-go traffic, all-you-can-eat buffets... Chuckle to yourself as Jesus steps in to help shut down that "body of death."

Triple Dare—Ever wanted to go skydiving? Do it! Catch one of the above, then plan it today and follow through. Naturally you'll need a buddy or two to do it with you.

Before the mountains were born
or you brought forth the whole world,
from everlasting to everlasting you are God.

Psalm 90:2

Watch That First Step

Following Christ is terrifying and exhilarating
Read Matthew 24:9-14 and John 11:8-16

I forgot to pull the rip cord—the cord that deploys the parachute. Yep, awesome. So it's a really good thing that I was skydiving tandem. I didn't really mean to go skydiving at all. It was an accident. My cousin had been telling me about his skydiving trip and I said, "Oh, I've always wanted to do that."

"When are we going?" he asked me. Hold it. Pause. Rewind.

"What? No." My words picked up momentum as I spoke. "The truth is that I really wanted to go when I was a kid, and then, just as soon as I turned eighteen, the desire to skydive mysteriously disappeared." He grinned at me. "So, when are we going?"

Six months later, it turned out, was the answer. Reality didn't set in until I climbed into a really unflattering green-and-black jumpsuit.

Then I met my tandem partner. He cracked jokes about how it was his first jump, too. Encouraged by my straight-man responses, the teasing became a running gag. When we climbed into the plane, I saw that everyone else had goggles. "Where are my goggles?" I demanded.

"Uh...shoot," he said. And though I knew he was messing with me—I was 89% sure that he was only messing with me—I wanted my darn goggles.

We climbed into the plane through a miniature version of a garage door behind the co-pilot's seat. There was not even a formal cockpit—only two chairs for the pilots. The plane, about as wide as my dining room table is long, had no seats. We shuffled in and sat back-to-front in two rows of thrill-seeking people, straddling the person in front of us. Tandem Man clipped my back to his chest with four locking carabiners. It was a mild reassurance that he was actually taking it seriously.

Within moments, I was distracted by the view as we climbed in altitude. I shuddered when I realized the manner by which I would be exiting the plane. I took slight comfort from my position at the back of the line.

That comfort didn't last long.

The door at the back of the plane opened and people started disappearing. The goggles that Tandem Man passed over my shoulder provided zero comfort. He pressed me forward toward the opening and my cameraman nonchalantly hung sideways outside the door of the plane. The absurdity of his casual air momentarily distracted me from reality.

Then I looked down. Thirteen THOUSAND feet down.

Never look down.

I tried to muster the gumption to jump, really, but on the video you can hear me yelling, "Oh, no! What am I doing?" My cousin, next in line, chomped at the bit. Because he's nuts. I didn't realize that I was gripping a metal bar above the door with iron fingers until I felt Tandem Man's stronger hands uncoiling mine.

Then I looked down. Thirteen THOUSAND feet down.

The ground was so far away. I wasn't ready, wasn't ready. But Tandem Man jumped, and I was attached to his chest with four carabiners, so I "jumped" too.

Then I was free-falling.

For. Seven.THOUSAND. Feet.

A mile and a half in less than two minutes.

And it was awesome.

The wind sounded like rushing water in my ears. The uplift pushed back so mightily it didn't seem like we were descending at all. I relaxed.

I smiled for Camera Man and soaked in the view of the world beneath me, so preoccupied that I forgot to pull the rip cord. Good thing Tandem Man wanted to live. When my body jolted upward, I belatedly thought, oh, yeah, the parachute.

Seriously.

When I say it's a miracle that I'm still alive, I'm only partly kidding.

Rushing waters, a jolt upward and then the most peaceful silence I have ever experienced, followed by the jubilation of realizing I would live. I tucked up my feet as the ground came forward to meet us and we slid to a stop. NOS-like adrenaline surged through me. I spun around and sprinted toward my cousin, who'd just landed and was running toward me.

"I want to do that again!" I shouted. He laughed.

For it has been granted to you on behalf of Christ, not only to believe in him, but also to suffer for him.
Philippians 1:29

I've never understood this verse and I have even less appreciation for what I think it's saying. The world's opposition of Christ is so fierce that, essentially, if we are suffering on behalf of Christ, then we are on the right track? Where do I sign up?

This is much the attitude of Thomas when he says, "Let us also go, that we may die with him" (John 11:16). Jesus wants to return to the city where people had very recently made an attempt on his life. The disciples stand at a crossroads. Will they follow Jesus, even knowing the risks?

Following Christ feels much like jumping out of an airplane. "Oh, no! What am I doing?"

It is frightening and exhilarating. Watch your step. That first one's a doozy. For the sake of Christ, I have walked away from dating relationships and detrimental friendships, have turned down jobs, moved across the country from people I love, and sacrificed more time, money, sweat and emotion than I have ever cared to keep track of.

I'm not alone, right?

Following Christ feels much like jumping out of an airplane.

Do you remember specific moments in your life when choosing Christ meant saying no to something else, something incredibly appealing? Which option did you choose?

It's a good thing Jesus never ever asked us to jump alone. We are tethered to him with a love more powerful than any man-made metal. And even though there are days when I am certain he is laughing at me, I know and trust with 89% of my heart that he knows what he's doing.

That's right—89%. I'd be lying if I said my whole heart. I doubt sometimes, and also fear. What scares *you* most about going "all in" for Christ?

God is in the process of making me perfect, but he still has quite a bit of work to do.

In the meantime, he's got my back and all I need to do is let him pry me away from safety—and enjoy the ride.

31

Dare—When's the last time you experienced the thrill of following Jesus? Say "no" to something in your life today (TV/ movie/ going out with the guys) and do something unsafe with Christ instead. Take a drive by yourself, radio off, and think through a specific idea that's occurred to you while doing these devos.

Double Dare—Do something unsafe with Christ. Visit a shut-in in their home, or a buddy in the hospital, or someone stuck rehabbing an injury. Be prepped to bring magazines, a good book, or Season 1 of something on DVD, to help them pass the time.

Triple Dare—Do something unsafe with Christ. Figure out the logistics and then go visit someone in jail. Friend, stranger, anybody. Be prepped to talk football, current events, stories about your kid's baseball league. Anything that will encourage or bring a smile. When they ask why, you say, "Jesus wanted me to do it."

Trust God from the bottom of your heart;
don't try to figure out everything on your own.
Listen for God's voice in everything you do,
everywhere you go; he's the one who will
keep you on track.

Proverbs 3:5, 6 (MSG)

Breath-Hold and Needing God

Can we truly live without God?
Read Ecclesiastes 12:9-14

Ever hold your breath just for fun? No, not like a kid trying to get your way, but seriously, just to see how long you can? (Go ahead and try it. We'll wait...)

The typical person, at rest, will get about 45 seconds in and be done. At 60 seconds you are officially above average. Anyone hitting 90 seconds or more has probably had some training.

"Wait a minute, training to hold your breath?" you ask. Well, there are several disciplines that naturally create the side effect of your body more effectively using oxygen. Runners have more efficient lungs naturally, and anyone living at high altitude will get a boost, too.

That's why the U.S. Olympic Training Center is located in Colorado Springs, and athletes from around the country train here to reap the benefits of high-altitude fitness.

You can also employ tricks developed by free divers and stage magicians, some used by the likes of Harry Houdini long ago.

It's called "forced apnea" and is a discipline that involves super-saturating your lungs with oxygen at specific intervals, thus enabling you to hold your breath for longer periods of time. Like before you're locked in a safe and rolled into a river. Naturally you'll never want to try any of these stunts by yourself, especially in water.

Speaking of water, have you heard the latest science on open water survival? Remember those old theories about cold water immersion that said you'd die from hypothermia shortly thereafter? Well, it turns out that's not always the case. The new model revolves around a formula expressed as 1-10-1 that progresses through an incident, starting at the very first minute.

1 — That's one minute to survive your initial immersion, which can often be dramatic or dangerous.

10 — If you didn't bang your head or ingest water, you have your next ten minutes to get atop your boat, don your life vest, or come up with a long-term plan to wait for assistance before losing all fine motor skills and coordination in your hands.

1 — If you're still in the water (wearing a floatation device) and you tuck your legs and curl your arms around yourself, you will survive near the one-hour mark. While sailors long expected to die quickly in cold water, the new evidence says that a healthy adult with some fat layers can easily survive 45 minutes or longer in this position.

So you can easily survive for a minute without taking in air, and potentially up to an hour immersed in cold water. Got it.

How long do you think you can survive without God?

Trick question, maybe? He is, after all, the air we breathe (Acts 17:25), and all creation is created by him, for him, through him, and finds its meaning in him (Col. 1:16-17). We may say that life without God is not a good thing, but would our actions back this up?

How long do you think you can survive without God?

Do I really believe that "Man shall not live on bread alone, but on every word that comes from the mouth of God" (Matt. 4:4)? Quick test—how much time did any of us spend in God's Word this last week? If we honestly believe that more than air, more than warmth, we need our gracious Lord God to live, do our actions support this?

Okay, maybe I don't camp out in the pages of the Bible as much as I should. But if his Word truly is life-giving, shouldn't I?

It's not always easy. Not just because I'm distracted by the culture that surrounds me, but because it's genuinely hard for me to wrap my mind around the notion that reading God's Word leads to a better life. Read it and then follow it? That's the formula for the best life you and I could ever have?

Referring to Solomon, "Now all has been heard; here is the conclusion of the matter: Fear God and keep his commandments..." (Eccl. 12:13).

There it is. The best way to live, in a nutshell, and it's not about our jobs. Not about our degrees. Not about networking, eating right, or exercising daily, but about trying our best to know God's character and his ways, and then stepping out in faith to walk in them, each and every day, strengthened by his Holy Spirit at work in us.

And what happens when I fail to renew my mind by spending time in God's Word?

Try holding your breath for three minutes. Or maybe filling the bathtub with ice water and lying in it for two hours. The results are all the same. We slowly become less capable of responding to God, of living his ways, of reacting righteously within this fallen world.

And yet, his Word... Like a sharp inhalation, a flood of warmth through our bodies.

Is diving into God's Word each day going to be a life-giving habit that you invest in? A campfire where you can warm yourself before heading out into the cold, life-sapping world?

Or is it going to be a deep exhale when you simply can't hold your breath any longer...

Dare—There are six chapters in the book of Ephesians. Read any three chapters on any three days this week, then hold your breath as long as you can after. Try and find something in that chapter that you can ponder or come back to throughout the day. Note the impact at week's end.

Double Dare—As described above, read all six chapters in Ephesians, one per day, holding your breath after each time. Note the impact of it all at week's end.

Triple Dare—As described above, read all six chapters, finding something from each one to ponder throughout your day. Breath-holding too. Note the impact of it all at week's end, then share something you learned or discovered with your wife or trusted friend. You can impress them with your breath-holding, too.

Triple Dog Dare—Everything as described above, plus, challenge your Triple Dare person to hold their breath longer than you. Loser owes back-rub, ice cream or pizza.

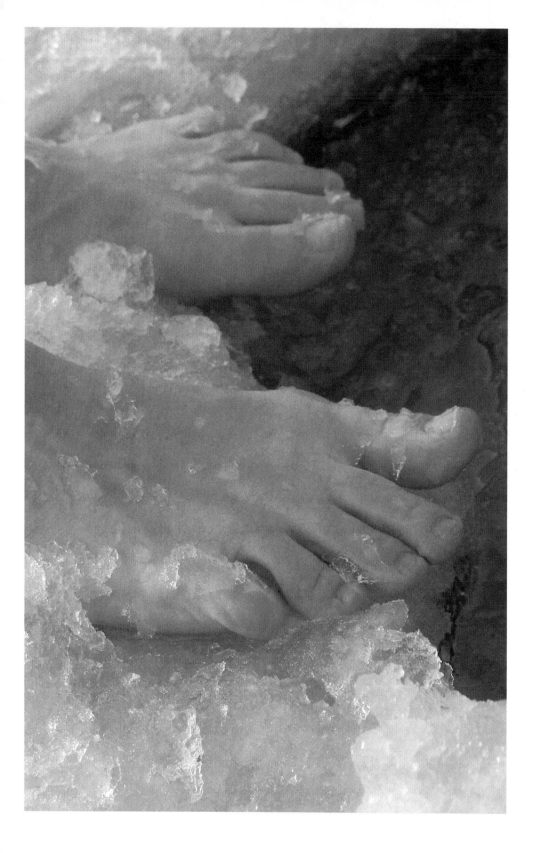

The Dumbest Thing
I've Ever Done

Peer pressure
Read John 8:2-11

Because another college student told me to do it. Because the sweetest, shyest girl in my hall had done it the year before. And if she can do it… Because if I did it, I would earn a T-shirt with a picture of a toilet plunger on it that said, "It takes a little more to be a plunger."

I could do an entire blog series on "Stupid Things Sam Has Done Because of Peer Pressure," but this was probably the dumbest. Welcome to Lake Johanna's annual Polar Plunge.

The students in charge of the event cut through two feet of ice to find water. The angry February sky gave the lake's surface a black appearance. The presence of an ambulance, just in case, caught me off guard. Then I shrugged it off. An ambulance made sense.

When I walked onto the edge of the ice, barefoot and wearing nothing but a swimsuit, I felt under-dressed, but only because one guy wore wings and several others wore capes with their swim trunks.

I silently gave my classmates props for having the ingenuity to tie a rope around my waist and that of my jumping buddy. It concerned me slightly that the rope idea hadn't occurred to me.

The guys tying the rope knew more about what would happen to me than I did. They tied the other end of the rope to the leg of a picnic table on the frozen lake. And then, in absolute true Sam fashion, while preparing to jump, I slipped on the blue tarp and fell, bringing my jumping buddy—whose hand I held—with me into the dark water of Lake Johanna.

My lungs seized instantly, and every limb declared mutiny at once. I tried to kick and stroke to the surface, but all I managed was a twitchy dog paddle. My face broke the surface and I pressed my palms to the tarp on the ice. I attempted to push up, but my arms declared strike. My jumping buddy appeared in my peripheral vision—also alive. As I clamped my hands around the leg of the picnic table, I felt a tug at my waist. One of the guys was pulling the rope.

That day, I became a member of the Polar Bear Club. It's the dumbest thing I've ever done.

My lungs seized instantly, and every limb declared mutiny at once.

They handed me a T-shirt—my trophy—and 45 seconds later I stood in a warming house.

The small private college I attended boasted strange peer pressures. Peer pressure to get your name spray-painted on a rock (long story), peer pressure to get married, peer pressure to jump into the lake through holes in the ice. There was also peer pressure to be holy.

The Pharisees, too, placed a peer pressure of holiness onto themselves and onto everyone around them. They convinced themselves that their motivations stemmed from loving and following God.

"When they kept on questioning him, he straightened up and said to them, 'Let any of you who is without sin be the first to throw a stone at her'… at this, those who heard began to go away one at a time, the older ones first, until only Jesus was left" (John 8:7, 9).

A shady situation to begin with, these men using a woman as bait to try and trap Jesus. Was it the scheme of only a few? How much persuading did it require to convince the rest? They dragged a woman into the street, shamed her, and, rocks in hand, fully intended violence, convinced they were justified in their actions.

Peer pressure—the urge to go along with the group—leads us to decisions that we would seldom make on our own. One individual, acting alone, would not have been so bold. The support of his colleagues granted him permission, gave him confidence and validation.

Jesus created a peer pressure to surrender.

But one voice, Truth, spoke up. It pierced through their joints and marrow, soul and spirit (Heb. 4:12) and jabbed at their hearts.

"Let any of you…without sin," Jesus' words cut through the fog of their schemes. One by one, we read, oldest first, they all woke up, and walked away. Jesus created a peer pressure to surrender.

Have you ever succumbed to peer pressure?

- Harassing or gossiping about a co-worker?

- Purchasing the latest and greatest hunting, fishing, rafting, climbing, or camping gear?

- Or the latest and greatest house, truck, camper, ATV, snow mobile or jet ski?

- Maybe drinking to excess?

- Making crude remarks to, or about, the opposite sex?

Whose voice are you listening to? Is your crowd submerged in a fog of unholy behavior? It only takes one strong voice of reason and truth to break through.

Be that voice.

_____

Dare—Compliment five different people today. Clothes, ideas, performance, hair, anything goes (be careful with the opposite sex, please).

Double Dare—Compliment 20 different people today. Cool webpage, nice car, great T-shirt…you know how it goes (be careful with the opposite sex again, please).

Triple Dare—While running the Double Dare, prayerfully ask God to send you an opportunity to stand up for an underdog. In faith, go through your day looking closely for this opportunity—and take immediate action. Someone's opinion shot down? Someone being harassed, pushed aside, or taken advantage of? Agree with them, stand with them, help them up. Be Christ to someone in need today.

Stiff-Finger Knots and Having a Plan

Sexual temptation: it's just a matter of time
Read Genesis 39:1-20

When I teach Swiftwater Rescue Courses, one of the elements we train on is knots. Knot theory, good knots versus bad, various knots and their uses, and finally, how to actually tie them. Tie a Figure 8-on-a-bight and you're looking good, but that's not the end of it. No, to really be an expert rescuer, you need to be able to tell me a specific use for that knot, and then be prepared to tie it under a variety of adverse conditions.

Think about having to tie that very same knot without looking. It's also quite possible you'll have to tie a knot underwater, or at times when your fingers are likely to be cold and stiff.

The knot you cannot tie when you need to is absolutely no use at all. Planning and practicing tying knots ahead of time, in extreme situations, especially when you are impaired, is just good sense. Similarly, knowing ahead of time how to act in any situation where your ability to make God-honoring choices might be somewhat impaired is also just good sense.

For instance, do you have a plan for how to handle sexual temptation before it happens? Or do you reactively respond to each situation as it occurs? Take our good friend Joseph in today's verses.

Kudos, Joseph, for choosing to withdraw from the sexually tempting situation you found yourself in! No shame in just sprinting out the door. Nice and simple. But Joseph, Joseph... really? You left behind physical evidence that this woman could later use to cry foul and cast you as a villain? If you had only taken off a split-second earlier—before she had a chance to grab your cloak! Better yet, knowing this woman's intentions, why allow her to be alone with you at all, even for a moment? If you had kept a buddy around, she would never have had the opportunity to lie or cause you trouble.

Reactive response vs. a well-planned, well-timed, and well-executed response. This isn't amateur hour, people! Joseph did the right thing, and was totally justified, but still ended up going to jail.

43

Personally, I like the ease and simplicity of the "second person plan" (a.k.a. a wingman) in any workplace or group setting.

In explaining our church's "never alone with kids, or the other gender" policy to our volunteer hiking guides, I share that it's not that we don't trust them. Exactly the opposite, really. By always having a second person around, if anyone—a parent, another adult, some Egyptian hottie—should ever accuse one of my guides of something, *anything*, all they have to do is casually reply, "Go ask Bob... he was there." And that's it. No wordy explanations. No long defense. Case pretty much closed. The other person being there *is* your defense. You're completely secure.

Flee from sexual immorality ... honor God with your bodies.
1 Corinthians 6:18-20

Now we may not always have the option to travel in "packs" with others, or have a trusted friend available 24/7, but we can at least identify the areas we would want that person in place and make plans before we even get there. Some of the classics:

Solo travel. I have a speaker friend who always travels with a buddy to his talks. Period. Must be nice being one of his friends, because you never know when it'll be your turn to be his "assistant" and fly out to Colorado Springs for the weekend. Yet, for the price of a second airline ticket and double hotel room, this guy will never, *ever* have to worry about falling for some hottie in the hotel bar, going out to a strip club, or failing to turn the TV channel past something he shouldn't be watching.

Padding the expense report. Simple, run it by someone else to verify before you turn it in. If they find an error, you owe them lunch. This could even be your kid if you want to show a teenage boy what ethical behavior really looks like. Ask your assistant to go through everything with a fine-tooth comb.

Dating problems. You won't be horizontal together and clothes will never come off if you only plan in advance to never be alone at each other's places. This need not be a rule in everyday hanging out, but you *know* when it's dangerous and an advance plan to keep it social makes all the difference. And what about having an exit strategy? In this connected world, it's simplicity itself. Have your wife call you at a time when you'll be done with dinner and potentially sitting around bored, looking for something to do.

When in doubt, 8:30 pm local time works nicely. Not married? Have a trusted friend call you, same deal. Trusted friends only, please, no flakes.

Buddies heading out to the strip club and stopped by to invite you? Ha, toss your wife/friend/whomever under the bus! "Sorry, guys, I was just about to call my wife. Have fun without me!" Feeling lonely and your cute fellow traveler is paying too much attention to you across the hotel hot tub? Same deal—"Sorry, gotta call my wife in a few minutes. You were saying?" Situation totally defused!

All circumstances will differ, but you get the general idea. Pray for wisdom, strength, and have a plan. Again, with all due respect to our brother-in-faith, Joseph, having to sprint away from the problem after the gal in question already has her mitts on you sounds like poor initial planning and a last-second exit strategy.

Let's learn from our fellow believer's mistake and create an exit plan. Praying and spending time in God's Word also protects us.

Worst case scenario, we have our running shoes laced tightly, so that whenever we are in a place where temptation lies in wait, hoping to entice us, we can confidently stride, or sprint, right on past, laughing at the pitiful attempts of the Enemy to snare us.

Avoid a reactive response with a well-planned, well-timed, and well-executed plan.

Dare—Have a wingman? A buddy you can travel with who helps keep you out of trouble? Anyone that can call you nightly at a prearranged time? Get one.

Double Dare—No wingman? Still no problem, with a few alterations. Use your laptop only in the public areas of the hotel. No hanging out near the pool area without reason. Always have a return time if going out to dinner. And of course, doing devos and reading the Word while traveling works wonders.

Triple Dare—Remember, you can always call *them* too. Easy plan? Call at 10:00 pm and tell them where you are. Anything but, "in my hotel room, in my jammies" means you owe them $50. Same for no call. Same for any excuses. Don't know about you, but that would help keep me out of trouble.

The Undertow of Sin

The effects of our choices
Read Numbers 22:21-33 and 23:5-12

Nausea, vomiting, fever, chills, muscle cramps, tremors, paralysis, fainting, seizures, elevated heart rate, and decreased blood pressure may develop. Death may even occur." According to WebMD, this is what could have happened to me if I had impulsively stepped down.

Arriving in the Bahamas, we drove past a bright yellow water tower painted like a smiley face. I have blurred impressions of hundreds of people dancing in the street, of lights and laughter, and steel drum music. That first night I watched a man limbo beneath glass Coke bottles.

The next day I went snorkeling with my dad, with the white beach to our left, and the sparkling aquamarine expanse to our right. We did our best not to kick up sand beneath us as we waded into the four-foot-deep water.

My shallow trust in the snorkel further diminished each time I allowed the opening at the top to dip below the surface. I struggled to get it right and, frustrated, I stood on the ocean floor several times just to breathe with my face above water, the way God intended.

Eventually, however, I got the hang of it and floated near the surface, peering at the strange, grainy world beneath me. I even saw a few fish.

By the time I saw the body of the stingray, it was directly beneath my own.

But I freaked out at what I saw next. It came from behind and below, so that by the time I saw the body of the gray stingray, it was directly beneath my own.

My heart dropped. My snorkel tipped beneath the surface. My body's first instinct was to get my feet under me, stand upright and find my breath.

Do not step on the stingray. It was a single, punctuated thought that erased every other.

I managed to stop my legs in mid-motion and bring my heels back up toward the water's surface. In the seconds that followed, I watched, awestruck, this creature manufactured by God's sense of humor.

Can you imagine the vastly different outcome, had I surrendered to my gut impulse and stepped down?

Both the righteous and the foolish are categorized by their decisions.

Decisions define us. The Bible's pages are filled with righteous men and women who step out in crazy faith, as well as foolish men and women who step out with a single-minded selfishness.

The righteous and the foolish are both categorized by their decisions. If we follow the Lord, being led by the Holy Spirit, then our decisions reflect that.

The prophet Balaam rode toward a large payout by the king of Moab—all he had to do was curse God's blessed people—when his donkey suddenly refused to walk any farther (Num. 23-24). Balaam kinda-sorta knew about God, but in truth, he was a "prophet for profit."

Similar to modern-day psychics, Balaam dabbled in powers beyond his comprehension. So God placed a warrior angel in Balaam's path and a true, righteous fear of the Lord in Balaam's heart. Balaam's heart did a complete 180. When the king told Balaam to curse the Israelites, Balaam forfeited his payday, risked the king's wrath and, instead, blessed the Israelites. Selfishness thwarted, Balaam risked his life and stepped out in crazy, righteous faith.

Can you see the difference in the decisions and their outcomes? One pleases self. One pleases God. You can't please both.

Balak said to Balaam, "What have you done to me? I brought you to curse my enemies, but you have done nothing but bless them!"

Numbers 23:11

48

Balaam is defined in history by his decisions. The world around us is shaped by our decisions.

But as with me that summer, there is danger; death may even occur, if we impulsively choose our own way. The undertow of sin is death, and choosing wisely is a moment-by-moment decision. Watch your stroke. Balaam's allegiance to God may have been short-lived, because forty years later he was killed by the Israelites among their enemies (Josh. 13:22).

My most natural instinct is for myself. The godly decision follows close behind, but is usually much more difficult.

Ever had to sacrifice a "payday" for the gospel? May God reveal to each of us the pitfalls that lie before us, and give us an enduring strength to overcome them all.

―――――――――

Dare―Read Numbers 22-24, Deuteronomy 30:11-20, and/or Romans 7:7-25. How are you applying these principles to your daily life? Ask church leaders about where you could offer help.

Double Dare―Coordinate with a church leader to help a widow or single mom for four hours one day, along with some friends. Yard work, cleaning gutters, or anything with "hard to do" written on it is fair game.

Triple Dog Dare―Same, but invite a group from church to join you. Blow an elderly widow's mind. Send a few single moms out to Chick-fil-A® for a few hours while your men's group takes their kids fishing.

Practice Makes Perfect

What am I practicing in my thought-life?
Read Mark 7:14-23

As the old adage suggests, practice makes perfect, and I can attest first-hand to this being true when it comes to the art form that is knot-tying. Some basic keys to understanding knots are as follows:

- **The knot should be easy to tie**—nothing that takes five minutes or requires tools.
- **The knot should stay tied**—tension knots need exactly that, friction knots don't.
- **The knot can be easily untied**—no Gordian knots here (google it).
- **The knot needs to be recognizable**—please don't tie your "Indian monkey's fist" and then look at me funny because I don't untie it simply by pulling the hidden loop.
- **The knot should not overly reduce the strength of the rope**—unlike the beloved bowline knot, which everyone learned in Boy Scouts, and can tie with one hand, but reduces rope strength by 50% at the site of the knot.

The water knot. The alpine butterfly. The full family of figure-8s, including on-a-bight, bunny ears, and with two uneven loops. I know and love them all, but that is not to say that I picked them up overnight. Not even close. Luckily, the secret to learning knots is simple. Once you get it, you tie it over and over again.

Practice after work, possibly during work, and sometimes even in your car at stoplights. There is no place that the simple routine of tying the in-line figure-8 will not work to cement that handful of strong, yet beautiful soft curves into your memory.

So what other habits can cement themselves in us, simply by practicing them over and over in our minds? Dropping F-bombs? Telling off other drivers in traffic snarls? Snapping at our wives, children, or co-workers?

We take captive every thought to make it obedient to Christ.
2 Corinthians 10:5

Has anything snuck into my words and actions specifically because I've unintentionally been practicing it in my thought-life for so long? How about voicing my frustrations at other drivers, or giving extended glances to women as they pass by?

Now let me offer a serious question—is there anything I've been doing solely in my head that I'm actually considering acting on? Having a tryst with a co-worker, telling off my boss, or letting the next person to annoy me really have it? None of which have any place in a true Christ-follower's heart or mind.

"Nor should there be obscenity, foolish talk or coarse joking, which are out of place, but rather thanksgiving" (Eph. 5:4). Our language is meant to be encouraging to others. Our tongues intended to edify, to build up, not to tear down. Yes, we've all done it—thought about how good it would feel to just let those words out. Turned the thoughts over and over in our minds, imagining just how powerfully those around us would be set straight, put in their place, and properly scolded for our perceived slights. Seriously?

"What causes fights and quarrels among you? Don't they come from your desires that battle within you?" (James 4:1)

Spinning butterfly kicks for slow people in the drive thru aside, how about if we pare these thoughts down to what they really are? Sinful attitudes sure, but thoughts like these are also just distractions.

Distractions that prevent me from truly loving my wife. That keep me from being a better team member or boss. That hinder me from getting more involved in my church. That get in the way of my having the Christ-like attitude I should towards the hurting people in the world around me.

Am I wasting time and mental resources entertaining thoughts that I will either never say or do, or more likely *shouldn't* ever say or do? What if I put that mental energy towards a better end?

Whatever is true, whatever is noble, whatever is right, whatever is pure, whatever is lovely, whatever is admirable—if anything is excellent or praiseworthy—think about such things.
Philippians 4:8

What if I repeatedly practiced exactly how to go about blowing my wife's mind with something I said or did? Something so loving, caring, and endearing, that she would absolutely melt with delighted surprise. Can you see it?

Quick question—how does it feel tossing that particular thought around inside your head?

Practice makes perfect, gents. It's true of knot tying, it's true for free throws, and you can only imagine what else in your life it's either helping to make amazing, or hindering completely.

Dare—Have a look at the list below. Pick any three and have some fun setting your mind on things that will benefit others.

Double Dare—Pick any five off the list below. Try and hit them all today. At least one must occur without other people's knowledge.

Triple Dare—Pick any seven off the list below. Try and hit them all in whatever remains of this week. At least one must occur without other people's knowledge.

List of Dare Activities:

- Next ride-share, offer your car.
- Next event, offer your time.
- Next need, offer your money.
- Make brownies for the Bible study, unexpectedly.
- Order pizza for the guys, unexpectedly.
- Make breakfast for your family unexpectedly.
- Bring donut/bagels for your team at work, unexpectedly.
- This week, log every time you say "No, but…" compared to "Yes, and..."
- Call your mom, tell her thanks for something.
- Call your wife, tell her thanks for something.
- Call your kiddo, tell them thanks for something.
- Make a list of God's goodness to you for this day, this week and/or this month. Email it to yourself.

Diamonds Aren't This Girl's Best Friend

The downhill slope of sin
Read Genesis 4:1-10

Frozen nose, ears and cheeks.
Steamed up glasses.
Stiff, red fingers.
Numb thighs and toes.
Frosty air that takes your breath away.
I *despise* being cold.

It should not surprise you, then, when I tell you that I have never acquired an affinity for downhill snow skiing.

Why would I subject myself to that, when I could be inside by a fireplace, with a mug of hot chocolate, reading a perfectly good book—an adventure-themed devotional perhaps?

You and I have that same insane lust for adventure, and I would keep pace with you almost anywhere. But you would lose me if you used the words snow, downhill and skiing in the same sentence.

I went skiing with friends once. No one taught me that pointing your skis together helped you slow down. Nor did anyone explain that cutting back and forth across a slope—as opposed to shooting straight down, also helped. On the easier slopes, those skills weren't necessary. Up 'til that point, my *modus operandi* had essentially been point and shoot. I'd fly down a slope with skis pointing straight down and pray that no one would cut in front of me. It was the most terrifying, energizing, and incredible (if I'm being honest) feeling in the whole world.

But I am not the greatest listener. And I usually don't waste my precious time with ridiculous things like *instructions*, when it is so much easier and faster to figure something out myself. So, if anyone had tried to explain the diamond's color significance, I absolutely, completely missed it. So did my friend.

55

We found ourselves at the top of a black diamond hill littered with trees. And I didn't know how to steer, or cut back and forth, or point my ski tips together—I had nothing in my tool belt to help me slow down.

My let's-turn-back-this-is-a-bad-idea button was damaged in utero. Not once did it occur to me that I could turn around.

To complicate the situation further, my let's-turn-back-this-is-a-bad-idea button was damaged in utero. So, not once did it occur to me that I could turn around. The decline was more freefall then slope. He and I stared down the dangerous chute where the sun glinted off the slick ice. Then we looked at one another with snowball-sized eyes. If he wasn't going to back down, neither was I. We shoved off.

Mmmm.

P=MV, right? Momentum equals mass times velocity.

Our ski tips hovered over the edge, momentum propelled me downward, and I froze with fear. More than anything, I wanted to rewind the past fifteen seconds. But, the decision had been made, and there was no turning back.

The memory of the bottom of that run is locked up tight in the let's-never-do-this-again corner of my brain. I have not downhill skied since, and it's been more than a decade. Years later, I inadvertently learned methods of slowing down that don't involve throwing shoulders into the snow.

Huh. The knowledge almost motivated me to try again. Almost.

That run stole my joy of downhill skiing.

If I had listened, and paid attention to the instruction, if I had admitted my fears, if I'd asked for help or advice, or simply said, "no" at the final stopping point, my experience would have been very different.

Once we start down a certain path, it's difficult to stop.

Trapping ourselves in sin shares similar qualities to my skiing episode. Once we start down a certain path, it's difficult to stop. Sometimes impossible. And it steals our joy. (That's why Satan's referred to as a thief.)

"Then the Lord said to Cain, 'Why are you angry? Why is your face downcast? If you do what is right, will you not be accepted? But if you do not do what is right, sin is crouching at your door; it desires to have you, but you must master it'" (Gen. 4:6-7).

How's that for a warning? Cain is entertaining murderous thoughts. God sees his heart and steps in. "Sin is crouching at your door..."

But sin is a slick, downward slope, and Cain had already stared down the run. He surrendered to the pull of evil that clawed at him. The momentum of his thoughts gripped him, propelling him forward. And then, Cain killed his brother.

Is there is a desire that ensnares you? Is it lust? Addiction to food or television? Alcoholism? Financial dishonesty? So often, we flirt with the origin of our sin at the top of the slope. We inch forward, lured by the wrongdoing that so easily entangles. Sin is crouching at your door. It desires to have you, but you must master it.

I have found myself faced with unbearable, alluring, enticing temptations—impulses that I *want* to give in to. Haven't you?

Here's a formula I've used to regain freedom from temptation. And, the more irresistible the longing, the more reluctant I am to begin. Because that first prayer sets everything in an upward motion. I know that when I beg God for help, God will come through—even when I don't want him to.

$C=P+V$. Change equals prayer and voice.

Pray. Voice your situation to someone else. And fail-safe: turn and run.

———

Dare—Put on the calendar a day to go sledding or snow skiing with friends or family.

Double Dare—Come as close as you can to walking through snowy woods at dusk. Bundle up and think of a recurring sin in your life. During your walk, come up with a practical plan to avoid it, combat it, or completely overcome it.

Triple Dare—Tell a trusted friend (not your wife) about this plan, sharing full details and goals. Give them permission to periodically check-in on your status.

Rappelling and Change Management

Both can be a bit unnerving
Read Ecclesiastes 3:1-11

Change is tough. Transitions are tough. New job, new school, new relationships, they all come with the requisite learning curve as you develop a sense of where the boundaries are and how to make the most of the new opportunity.

When rappelling, you find yourself in a similar situation, although in this case, the transition involves leaning back and stepping off the edge of a sheer cliff. Just as in life, this can be a bit tricky.

The rules, then, are simple—feet, brake, and free hand.

Your feet should be wide apart and both planted solidly on the rock face. Your brake hand should hold the trailing rope back along your hip, avoiding the temptation to let the rope draw your hand forward and get caught in your belay device. Ouch!

Last, your free hand helps you feel more stable, holding the rope in front of your face as you descend. Unlike your brake hand, this one will never grab the rope tightly. It simply slides along, ready to use if you take a wrong step or lose your footing.

The key is in staying loose. Flat hand against the rope (tostada) is fine, curved slightly (taco) is okay, but burritos (curled tightly) will only lead to friction burns and are not allowed.

Much can be gained by employing these rappelling principles to life's transitions. Staying flexible, fully committing to the change, and applying some Mexican food can all ease the transition and get you back to your peak performance.

Put another way—commit, relax, and look ahead.

Let's look at some of the biblical wisdom concerning change—with the apostle Paul and Jesus as our guides.

Forgetting what is behind and straining toward what is ahead, I press on toward the goal to win the prize for which God has called me heavenward in Christ Jesus.
Philippians 3:13-14

The reality of change is that, most often, you can't go back. Once over the edge on a rappel the only way is down, so you might as well get comfortable with it. Similarly, there's a lot to say for Paul's advice on committing to the path ahead, and not stressing about what you're leaving behind. Even Jesus confirms this when he replies to a potential follower, "No one who puts a hand to the plow and looks back is fit for service in the kingdom of God" (Luke 9:62). I guess nobody can "plow straight" when looking over their shoulder.

Along with this commitment to change is staying loose. Flexible. One possible mantra in your life's new surroundings? "Let's give it a try…"

Back to rappelling for a sec. Once you are past the edge and hanging vertically off the cliff, no matter how nervous you are, no matter how quickly your heart is beating, you will soon realize that the hardest part is over. Everything about the experience just got really easy, like law-of-gravity easy.

Even better, one of the most fun parts of rappelling is now available to you if you're willing to try. Give a short hop out away from the rock, let a length of rope slide through your brake hand, then lock off and swing back in, landing with your feet firmly under you. Laugh and repeat. Within seconds, you're jumping and sliding down the side of a cliff, just like SWAT teams in the movies.

Whether it's a new address, new job or new baby, at some point the boxes are unpacked, the new workstation set up, and life starts to find a new rhythm.

If you haven't already, it's a good time to look ahead and look around you, asking, "How can I make the most of this new opportunity?"

- What benefits are available to you here and nowhere else?
- What cool toys or fun experiences do you suddenly have access to?
- What wisdom, knowledge, or stories of life experience have just opened up to you?

I'm not talking about dental benefits and a nice view of the park. I'm asking about doors that have never been open to you before. People, thoughts, and opinions you've never heard until now. Opportunities to take advantage of that will charge up your imagination and potentially change your world, if you'll only take a deep breath, step out in faith, and ask.

You can't plow straight when you're looking over your shoulder.

Sometimes it takes a bit to get used to the new attitude, circumstance, life stage that you're in. But please don't make the mistake of hanging motionless and frightened on the side of the cliff, focused solely on wanting to go back where you just were. There's fun and excitement to be had farther along and going back up is simply not an option.

So yes, the transition is indeed the hard part, but afterwards? Something new and magical has opened up and it's up to you to go out and explore it. Leave the past behind, and look forward to God's next chapter in your life.

Are you ready?

Dare—Go through the list of "times" in Ecclesiastes 3:1-11 as a checklist. Try to remember a specific instance when you found yourself in just such a time. Any stand-outs? Lessons learned? "A time to dance" should be good for a laugh...

Double Dare—Little things can remind us that change is not to be feared. Go get lost. On a new trail. Take a new way home from church. Understand that the nervous feeling that comes with "different" is not such a big deal after all.

Triple Dare—Purposely seek out a change you've been putting off, or assist someone in the middle of theirs. Help a friend move. Help your wife re-arrange the furniture, just because... Catch up on something you've been letting go—clothes, hugs to your kids, salad dressings...

The Last Fire I Started Was in my Kitchen

Passion for Christ
Read Matthew 3:11-12

"The fire must be kept burning on the altar continuously. It must not go out" (Lev. 6:13).

The last fire I set was unintentional. And it was in my kitchen.

It started easily enough. Add unseen char from a previous meal with a distracted mother of three, and you get an actual, legit fire. I swiftly doused the nine-inch flames with baking soda.

That moment stands in stark contrast to a canoe trip, when a friend challenged/dared me to start a fire with flint and magnesium. My friend had a lighter in his pocket, but he only smirked when I asked for it. Instead, he passed me a bag of dry tinder. Helpful. My expression said as much, too.

I drew my knife from its sheath and pulled out a keychain with flint on one side and magnesium on the other. I brought it in case of an emergency, and also because I felt cool carrying it. I had no intention of *using* it. Muttering to myself, I knelt on the compact dirt, small pebbles digging into my kneecaps. I scrunched the tinder into a tiny pile and, with the knife, scraped shards of magnesium off of the keychain. I flipped the flint side up, expelled a breath, and mentally prepared to start that fire. I didn't actually believe it would work. Another friend took pity and knelt across from me, cupping his hands around the tinder. Lowering the flint until it hovered just above the kindling, I scraped the steel blade of the knife against the flint. Sparks flew fairly easily. The trick was getting one of them to stick.

And then, one did. It took a good ten to fifteen minutes and within that time span I had plenty of second thoughts and self-doubt. The spark became one small, single ember—fragile and precious. Breathe too hard on it and it would disappear. Nurturing the ember into a flame was more diffi-cult than creating it had been. I held one tiny twig up to the ember and blew so, so gently.

I have never been more proud of a two-inch flame in all my life. We ate dinner off that fire.

"The fire must be kept burning on the altar continuously. It must not go out" (Lev. 6:13).

God is giving Israelites instructions regarding burnt offerings. *Why* does God tell the Israelites to burn the sacrifice all night long? Well, ten verses later we read, "Every grain offering of a priest shall be burned com-pletely; it must not be eaten" (Lev. 6:23).

Perhaps, then, we can conclude the same regarding the burnt offering. In order to ensure that the ox burned to the point of being inedible, it stayed in the flames all night long. Regardless, the expectation is clear. The fire must not go out.

I like to start fires, be warmed by them, and lose my thoughts in their flames. I have melted plenty of shoe soles by standing too close.

Tending fires require a great deal of work. They must be watched con-stantly. Wood must be added and sometimes repositioned, the embers oc-casionally stirred. So when God commands that the fire not go out, the un-derstanding is that the offering will require someone watching it at all times—all through the night.

In Matthew 5:14, Jesus says we are the light of the world. It's not a la-bel we should wear carelessly. It is, and always will be, a sacrifice to be branded with the name of Christ. And just like the Old Testament sacri-fices, the flame must be constantly tended to, lest it diminish.

Selfishness can smother a fire—or become the sacrifice, the fuel by which Christ purifies us.

While I would certainly never describe the Holy Spirit as small or frag-ile, oftentimes my own passion for Christ flickers and feels so frail that it wouldn't take much to extinguish it. Worry, distraction, self-doubt, and re-gret all vie to huff and puff and blow out this little light of mine.

Fires require a perfect balance of materials to burn and oxygen to feed the flames. The truth about the fire within us is that the more we follow Christ, the larger the flame grows. The selfishness and self-centeredness that would otherwise smother a fire become the sacrifice, the fuel by which Christ purifies us, while simultaneously using the flame as a beacon to draw others to him.

What would my life look like if, instead of limiting Jesus to lighting a single candle within me, I allowed him to set the dry ground all around me ablaze? How would the lives of those I meet be affected by a radiant, shining passion for Christ?

John the Baptist said "I baptize you with water but after me comes one whose sandals I am not worthy to carry. He will baptize you with the Holy Spirit and fire. His winnowing fork is in his hand, and he will clear the threshing floor, gathering the wheat and burning up the chaff with an unquenchable fire. He must increase. I must decrease" (Matt. 3:11-12, John 3:30).

Remember, "The fire must not go out."

That fire-starter you've got in your backpack, "Go Bag," or lying around in the garage? Grab it, plus a pie plate or cookie sheet (covered in foil so your wife doesn't kill you) and head to the backyard, or garage.

Dare—Light a simple fire using only your fire tool, tissues, and hand sanitizer.

Double Dare—Try the previous, then light a simple fire using only your fire tool, and some cotton balls smeared with petroleum jelly.

Triple Dare—Try the previous, then light a simple fire using only your fire tool and some lint from your dryer. Use this time to spark a conversation with a neighbor or buddy about either Jesus or your silly devotional book.

Medical and Work Doesn't Last

Nothing lasts forever...
Read Ecclesiastes 2:1-11, 17-23

O n a long enough timeline, nothing in this world is going to last. Not a thing, right down to bandaging a wound. Let me explain. If you're going to get a Wilderness Medical Certification, be prepared to hear many concepts you will later put to the test, along with this little gem: any time you wrap or dress an injury in the wild, be prepared to completely re-do it again within hours.

I put this training to the test on a rafting trip on the Colorado River through the Utah wilderness. We hiked up into an area known for petrified tree trunks. Which are amazing. No really, if you've never seen petrified trees, just trust me and give them a try sometime. Growth rings, along with texture and grain, still clearly visible in the dark rock. They are, at least the first time, absolutely fascinating.

Hiking back down to the river required that we negotiate a short climb, but in reverse. Jumping down one at a time, we prepared to continue when our last member took a tumble upon landing and came to a stop with her knee planted firmly in the jutting point of a small tree limb.

We safely evac'ed our patient down to the water, then seated her comfortably on a cooler where several of us went into action.

Few women have ever seen such single-minded attention from a group of men.

As one gent boiled water to sterilize instruments, I used a sterile safety pin to poke a tiny hole in a Ziploc bag. Once filled with water, I sealed it and then squeezed out a high-pressure jet of water that worked beautifully to irrigate and clean the wound.

We called it good, but the patient remarked that no, she could still see something white in the wound. "Uhm…that's your kneecap," I answered carefully.

"Oh. Okay!" she replied with a grin. What a trooper.

Ten minutes later, the wound was clean, dressed, and concealed beautifully under a loose gauze wrap. Nobody said it, but standing there in the growing desert heat, we were all pretty proud of our work.

Which lasted about three hours, after which the bandage had slipped and needed adjusting. We re-dressed and completely re-wrapped the wound. And again after dinner on a quiet sandbar. And again at bedtime.

Asking our patient to not move and disrupt our beautiful bandaging was obviously not working well. Someone remarked that rather than dressing everything *again*, slathering the wound in topical antibiotic and leaving it open to the air might be a good idea. We all quickly agreed.

If ever a promise was true of this earth, it is that nothing will last. Everything is breaking down, coming apart, or wearing out. Even amongst the things of heaven, we're told that knowledge and prophecy will pass away, leaving only love remaining in the end (1 Cor. 13:8).

What in my life, if it was taken away tomorrow, would leave me devastated?

And so we're instructed not to not hold onto anything too tightly. This, of course, is in direct contradiction to our culture's addiction to stuff. Hey, we all love the U.S., but if you think that's an unfair statement, just Google "storage units" for your zip code.

Shortly after Jesus shared the Beatitudes during the Sermon on the Mount, he went on to mention a great approach to our own stuff. In Matthew 6:19 he said, "Do not store up for yourselves treasures on earth, where moths and vermin destroy, and where thieves break in and steal."

Sounds good, but that's just our stuff. Not a problem if we get overly attached to our accomplishments, our reputation, our job title, or our family's appearance, right?

Consider how Jesus finishes his thoughts on the subject, saying "…for where your treasure is, there your heart will be also" (Matt. 6:21). He goes on to describe the failure rate (a nice, round 100%) when trying to love, hold, or esteem anything of this fallen world while also trying to love and serve God at the same time.

So while we are encouraged and cheered on to pursue excellence in our jobs and accomplishments, we are also cautioned to carefully keep them in the proper perspective, and to never let them get in the way of following God.

A fun and easy test to see if this has crept into in your life? Ask yourself, "What in my life, if it was taken away tomorrow, would leave me devastated? What would I shed a tear over if it was suddenly gone? My wife or family?" Perfect. "My job?" Caution. "My toys, house, or lovingly restored Mustang?" Uh-oh.

But that's just the stuff. What about my work? Am I drawing too much of my identity or satisfaction in life from my career?

Two more questions: "If my work and accomplishments were forgotten tomorrow, would I be depressed for more than a day? Could I confidently say it was all God's and I'm working for his glory alone, not my own?" Definitely a bummer seeing years of work flushed away, but hopefully we would all move on quickly and go grab pancakes.

Our work will not last. Our strength will fade. People and things will come into our lives, and just as quickly, they will go. Ultimately, anyone holding too tightly to whatever they have in this world is going to be disappointed.

So let's treat the stuff of this world—including our jobs— just like our last rental car. Enjoy it, appreciate it, use and treat it well, but when it comes time to hand it in, toss 'em the keys and move on to what's next.

Dare—Make a list of three things you enjoy. Go without one of them, one day each, over any three days this week.

Double Dare—Make a list of four things you enjoy. Go without one of them, one week each, for this entire month.

Triple Dare—Take your list of three things you enjoy. Go without one for an entire month, every month, for the next three months.

Triple Dog Dare—Take your list of three things you enjoy. Go without one for an entire month, every month, for the next three months. Ask your wife, family or a trusted friend to join you during one of these months.

Options to consider for the above Dares: soda, beer, or coffee, chocolate, or all sweets, watching TV or movies, going to the movies, reading magazines, sitting in your favorite chair, eating out, buying books, movies, or music, buying tech toys, buying coffee…

Fire-Making and Doing Good Work

Don't settle for good enough
Read Luke 12:22-34

S o, having just talked about the value of not getting too invested in stuff that ultimately won't last, let's take a moment and talk briefly about why some things are still worth doing.

Ever started a fire? Surely, but ever with just one match? Without a match? Maybe you're a pro with a flint and steel, or a fire piston. Or what about making a fire using something really old-school.

Like a bow drill.

We were on an overnight training trip in some far-off river canyon, and one of the gals had decided she wanted to learn the bow drill method of fire-making. One of our guide staff was a survival junkie and offered to set her up with all the necessary equipment.

We sat around the campfire that evening, listening to the "sawing" sounds of our colleague's attempts behind us. After 45 minutes of frustrated efforts, she called for a break.

I wandered over to the setup. "Just looking," I told my friend, crouching down to watch him demonstrate.

"Give it a try," he offered, stepping aside.

So I reached for the bow and started, well, drilling. *What was I possibly going to accomplish?* The previous gal had drilled furiously back and forth for maximum friction, but I drew my bow across slowly, using long, even strokes. (Think "playing the cello" rather than "sawing wood.")

And, note to self, apparently slower is better in this case, because my spindle was starting to smoke. A lot.

The guide leaned in. "Keep going, keep going!" Focused intently on the spindle and fire block, I sensed people crowding in around me.

"You've got a spark. Quick, tip it into your tinder pile!" I did, watching the tiny glow tumble onto a fluffy ball of cottonwood down.

"Now blow on it," he instructed. "No, no, gently...like a lover." He grinned.

Uhm? But I did. Smoke poured out of the ball of fluff.

"Quick, take it away from your face!" he laughed. Thankfully, I did. Not a second later, the smoking ball of fuzz burst into flame.

A cheer went up from the surrounding crowd as I placed my small blaze under some dry twigs that immediately caught and began to burn. Without intending to, I had just started a fire using nothing but two pieces of wood. I was thrilled with my success and grinning from ear to ear.

At least, until the gal who had initiated the whole affair walked back over to see what all the commotion was about.

Question: is there any good reason to pick up someone else's abandoned efforts, knowing their reaction is going to be surprise, anger, then immediate destruction of your efforts should you clumsily succeed where they didn't?

Glorifying God is in obedience to his Word, and not just for our annual review.

Is there any reason to give your all to a project that's going to be forgotten within weeks of completion? To a report that nobody is going to read? To a training talk that no one is really going to pay attention to and is only attending because HR made them?

Why go out of your way to put any effort into tasks that are seemingly meaningless and that ultimately won't last? Why? Because our Lord God loves it when we do good work.

"Whatever you do, work at it with all your heart, as working for the Lord, not for human masters, since you know that you will receive an inheritance from the Lord as a reward" (Col. 3:23-24).

But is there value in undertaking projects that seem to have no purpose, completing assignments that will probably affect no one at all?

Consider our creator God's approach to the question. In both Luke 12 and Matthew 6, we read that God delights in creating wildflowers, giving them beauty that surpasses kings, even though it's very likely that nobody will ever see them. Yet, still he takes joy in their creation.

"Walk into the fields and look at the wildflowers. They don't fuss with their appearance—but have you ever seen color and design quite like it? The ten best-dressed men and women in the country look shabby alongside them. If God gives such attention to the wildflowers, most of them never

72

even seen, don't you think he'll attend to you, take pride in you, do his best for you?" (Luke 12:25-28 MSG).

When we choose to take pride in creating, operating, maintaining, or any other role in this world, we join our heavenly Father in the very same work we see him spending his time and efforts on. To invest of ourselves and not simply pencil-whip our responsibilities shows a respect towards Scripture like Ephesians 6:5, asking us to "...obey your earthly masters with respect and fear, and with sincerity of heart, just as you would obey Christ."

Glorifying God is in obedience to his Word, and not just for our annual review.

In light of eternity, it's true; we're simply borrowing this temporary world: the tools, the talent, and the possibilities we live with. Nothing we make will last, but then, is that really a reason not to strive and make our heavenly Father proud while we're here?

Take pride in your work. Make the most of that task, even if it's thankless and will seemingly make little or no difference to others. Do it all with the glory of our Lord God in mind, and for his appreciation.

You and I never know when God is going to take our meager, half-hearted efforts and fan them into flames for all to see.

———————————

Call up some buddies; it's time to start more fires. Grab that cookie sheet again (still covered in foil) and head back to the backyard or garage.

Dare—Using only a flint striker and your choice from "Kitchen Fire" Dares, ignite a fire that will catch a finger-sized twig. (**Handy tip**—rather than strike the flint with the knife, hold the knife in place and rake the flint bar back and upwards against it. Fourth of July, baby...)

Double Dare—Using waterproof matches, ignite a fire that will catch a finger-sized twig using only snack-size corn chips (the fattier the better).

Triple Dare—Using only a flint striker, ignite a fire that will catch a finger-sized twig using only dryer lint saturated in paraffin/candle wax, jammed into either a toilet paper tube, a large straw, or egg carton material. Use this time to spark a conversation with a neighbor or buddy about some recent Dares that stood out to you in your silly devotional book.

Leeches on Beaches

Righteousness is gifted, not earned
Read 2 Kings 5:1-19

If you have ever spent an extended amount of time in the wilderness, you know there's a certain point when everything begins to smell the same—the fire, the water, your clothes and skin, the people you are camping with. There is an incredibly pungent outdoor odor that your nose becomes desensitized to after four or five days.

One summer when I was in college, after a camping trip with friends from church, I returned to my friend's parents' house to shower. He and I talked about all the foods we wanted to eat and how quickly we would fall asleep in *real* beds. I distinctly remember his mom turning toward us and saying, "But the first thing you're going to do is shower." Her comment surprised us. We couldn't smell what she smelled.

Bits of leaves and twigs fell to the floor as I shampooed my hair. It was a long time after that before I took a hot shower for granted again. When I unzipped my rucksack to do laundry, I smelled what my friend's mom had smelled—and reeled back and gagged.

Rewind to day three out on the river.

I could still smell myself and wanted to wash up. A lack of rain that year had resulted in low river levels, and a lazy current made wading out from shore through the muck an impossibility.

The brilliant plan: my friend and I would canoe out to the middle of the river.

Step 1: Jump from canoe without tipping it. I stood atop the seat, jumped more upward than outward, and my friend counterbalanced the abrupt motion. Success.

Step 2: Scrub hair while treading water in a river. Eh. Needs Improvement. But I got the job done.

Step 3: Swing legs onto side of canoe to check for leeches. (I hoped not to find any.)

I was certainly not supposed to find three.

Brown with a translucent quality, one was about an inch long and a centimeter wide. The other was much smaller—just a cute little baby leech learning the ways of the world. I tried to bank my panic.

"I have a knife," my friend offered.

"Do it." I replied. After he scraped them off the first leg, I pulled my second leg up.

He adjusted his grip on the knife.

Lather. Rinse. Repeat.

I performed crazy acrobatics in the attempt to wash myself—and honestly, the river wasn't even that clean. Plus, I ended up with leeches on my legs, and the clean feeling only lasted until the dinner fire.

He adjusted his grip on the knife.
Lather. Rinse. Repeat.

All that effort, and for what?

Just to recap your reading for the day (2 Kings 5:1-19), Naaman was a successful, highly regarded commander of the army of Aram. And he had leprosy. An Israelite captive who served Naaman's wife told her about the prophet Elisha, who could heal Naaman.

When Elisha met Naaman, he told him to wash in the Jordan seven times for his skin to be restored. But Naaman left angry, scoffing at Elisha's instructions to bathe in the filthy Jordan, having wanted to be cured with the wave of a hand. Naaman's servants encouraged him to listen to the prophet. So, Naaman did as Elisha instructed—and his skin was restored. Because of his healing, Naaman believed in God.

Naaman is commanded to bathe in the Jordan River seven times. To him, as it did to me, the process seemed a little out there. In his case, unlike in mine, the directive came from God. And in his case, unlike in mine, the action actually cleansed him.

I would have required more parameters:

How long should I scrub for it to count as a bath?

Should I use soap?

Is there a designated amount of time to wait on the shore before reemerging?

I often do the same thing regarding my spirituality:

I need to read my Bible for 45 minutes this morning.

I need to write in my thankful journal every day.

I need to pray for every single person I know tonight.

I should memorize Colossians.

Every time I swear, I'll put a quarter in a jar.

If I accomplish these feats by my own effort, then I will be spiritually clean, or so I think. In the end, I fail. But I set these standards. They do not come from God.

Our righteousness is not based on what we can do for God. Do you get that? Do you ever make the same mistake?

I have to _____.

I should _____.

I can't _____ anymore.

God has already sanctified us. Once we are made clean by the blood of Jesus, sin stops sticking. There is nothing we can do to earn our righteousness. And the thing is we don't have to. Through Christ, we already own it.

So, whatever sin is leeched onto you, whatever that thing is that you hate yourself for because it gets the best of you more often than you want to admit, whatever regrets weigh heavy on your heart—forgive yourself. Lay it at the cross where Jesus has already forgiven you.

Also, if you ever find yourself needing to wash your hair when the river is low, simply pour water over your head with a bucket while remaining in the boat.

———————

Dare—Find a river and skip stones (unless it's February in MN). For every skip you get, let go of something that weighs heavy on your heart. Example: Two skips: "I let go of my finances." "I release the anger I have about ____."

Double Dare—Consider the other guy's spiritual maturity. Rein in your freedom for his sake and watch the PG movie. Consider his finances. Pick up the check for him. Consider his pace. Be patient and go his speed on the racquetball court, in the conversation, etc.

Triple Dare—Plan a friends and/or family canoe trip. Put it on the calendar today. Bonus points for jumping from the canoe without tipping it.

Knowing Your Bible and Referring Visitors

Just how well do we know God's Word?
Read Romans 12:1-21

Every city has attractions that visitors want to experience when they stop in. If you're in DC, it's all about the monuments. Visiting the coast? Time to hit the beach! Memphis? Barbeque. Austin? Music. The list goes on and on. When you live in Colorado Springs, the requests tend to run towards, "Where's a good place to go hiking?"

And living in "The Springs" like me guarantees you'll see a lot of visitors on the trails. There are the tourists who flock to the area each summer, not to mention your own houseguests. Suddenly there you are, four hours until the next meal, and someone's asking, "Where's a fun, scenic place you'd recommend that's close by to take a quick hike?"

It is at this moment that you are defined as either a true resident of this wonderful city, or simply another visitor that chose to stay a bit longer than the others. What's the difference? One will send their friends up to a local canyon filled with waterfalls and quiet streamside trails. The other will draw a blank, and then reluctantly direct them to the congested traffic and over-crowded paved pathways winding through Garden of the Gods Park.

One person who really knows the city can show their friends its "locals only" secrets; the other falls back on a location known to any tourist with a guidebook. A spectacular setting, to be sure, but as someone fortunate enough to live year-round in a place where others come on vacation, I could at least point them to the unpaved hiking trails!

So which one would you be?

Next question—if it came to someone asking you a similar recommendation about God's Word, where would you fall?

Could you point out a Psalm that would apply to someone feeling glad? Or crushed? Could you point out a passage to capture the attention of someone who loves nature?

If someone wanted to dive into the Bible for the first time, which books or passages would you recommend? Which shorter book would you offer to get them started? Which ones are historical narratives and which ones talk about Jesus? You get the picture.

It's embarrassing to admit, but sometimes the people visiting our cities take far better advantage of the opportunities for fun than we do. In the same vein, have I taken the time to learn my way around God's Word to a level where I can point out relevant content to others, or am I sheepishly searching through the index to find a passage covering topics such as "relationship with my wife" or "freedom in Christ"?

Get to know your way around the Word.

Let's take a moment and toss out some ideas for these very questions. Snap a photo of the list below, and should they come up in the future, you're covered!

- What's a good Psalm when feeling happy? Try any of the Psalms around 30-40.

- What's a good Psalm when you've completely dropped the ball? Psalm 51.

- Which passages would capture a nature lover? Psalm 19, 104, and Isaiah 40.

- Which passage lays out a step-by-step guide on what love should look like? 1 Corinthians 13.

- What's a good short book to introduce someone to the Bible who's never read it before? Choose from Galatians, Ephesians, Philippians, or Colossians.

- Where's a great place to start reading the Bible from Day 1? Try a short Gospel, like Mark.

- Where's a good list of reminders for everyday living? Romans 12.

- Best examples of living our faith? Hebrews 11.

- Show me a reminder that I am free in Christ? Galatians 5, baby!

Take this list as just the start and make notes of your own. What's a good Old Testament story of courage you would share? Or an example of leadership?

Just as spending time outside exploring or playing in the location you call home will allow you to more readily share fun spots with your visitors,

80

the more you pour your time and attention into God's Word, the easier it will come to mind as well. Even obscure passages on marriage (1 Pet. 3:7, yikes!) and handling anxiety (Phil. 4:6-7) will spring to mind when needed.

Know that whatever you read through, whatever nuggets of wisdom you find, will likely make their way into conversations and other people's questions for you in the future. That's because our model of ultimate, objective Truth is both living and active and always waiting to be shared.

You never know when friends are going to drop in and want a great ice cream or gelato spot. You also never know when a friend is going to ask you, out of nowhere, "My buddy just got a new Bible and wants to know an easy place to start reading. What do you recommend?"

At these times, a good knowledge of the go-to spots in town, as well as in God's Word, is a truly wonderful thing to have.

And if you ever find yourself in Colorado Springs, be sure to have a look at these amazing spots, too:

- Best canyon hike along a stream? Seven Bridges

- Best views of the city? Tie, Mount Cutler Trail and Cheyenne Mountain Zoo

- Most scenic running trails? Garden of the Gods (the unpaved trails)

- Most scenic mountain biking trail? In town, Ute Valley Park, or just thirty minutes away, Rampart Reservoir Loop

———

Dare—Pick one or two of the cheat-sheet passages listed above and read it. Who can you pass it along to? Share your knowledge with others when asked.

Double Dare—That fun thing in your area that all the tourists do and you're still meaning to? Do the above Dare, then immediately put that fun thing on your schedule, first available opening.

Triple Dare—Do the Double Dare. Also, snap a photo, print out the cheat-sheet, and read each of the references listed. At the end, add any meaningful scripture passages that stand out to you. Make a note to read through these passages each month, until you can summarize them and list the verse reference. Again, look for opportunities to share this knowledge.

I Hate Running

I hate running. By the end of three miles, I am always red-faced, gasping like a fish out of water, and sweating so profusely that I look like I just stepped out of a pool.

When I lived in Oregon, I loved running on an unpaved path along the river. Because the woods were gorgeous, yes, but also because no one was there to witness my slow mutation into a crimson largemouth bass.

Sometimes, though, I ran the high school track to gauge my split times. One March afternoon, I arrived as the track team was clearing out. Being a youth director at the time, I noticed one of the teens from my church walking toward the locker rooms along with the rest of the team.

I hadn't been running for very long when I heard footsteps coming up fast behind me—the same young man I'd just seen. "Only 12 laps left to go," I muttered.

"We can do 12 laps," he replied. "Twelve laps are easy."

I glanced at him, wondering if he was actually planning to run all three miles with me.

"You...just...finished practice," I said, in between gasps for breath.

"I know. I was there. Anyway, it's not like you're running that fast. It will be a nice cooldown."

He darted to the right to avoid my slow motion elbow. I rolled my eyes at him, but he just laughed and returned to the lane beside me. And he stayed there for 11 more laps.

After that day, he often ran with me. I never had much breath to spare, but I found enough to grumble at him whenever he ran backwards in front of me, jabbering away with a cocky smile. Some days we did 16 laps just for—what he referred to as—fun.

Sometimes a friend of his joined us. He also enjoyed running backwards in front of me. It became a game that *they* very much enjoyed. I hate running.

I hate running, but by the end of May, after running with these guys for two months, I dropped 1:30 off my per-mile pace.

Each June in Lebanon, OR, there is a 5K—down Main Street and back —that ends just minutes before the annual Strawberry parade begins. Runners are cheered on by people lining up to watch the parade. One blistering-hot year, I entered the race.

The gun popped and the runners each found their stride. And there beside me appeared the teen from my youth group. I didn't see where he'd come from, and I looked pointedly at the front of his shirt and the absence of the paper race number. He grinned. I rolled my eyes, and we slightly upped our pace.

"Only 12 laps left," he said. People cheered our names from the curb, mostly teenage girls cheering for him.

About a half mile down the street sat his buddy, watching the parade with friends. In jeans and a polo shirt, he was not dressed to run.

"Come on!" my running partner called to him. I laughed. Like that was going to...but he hopped up and matched my stride. They flanked me, and elation increased my pace. They started in with their usual jokes, talking around me and running backwards to taunt me.

Just before the halfway point, I dropped to a walk. Disheartened, I surrendered my hope of a personal record (PR). After dragging air into my lungs for a few strides, I hopped back into a run and crossed the finish line well below my previous PR.

That young man from my church could have finished the race in less than 18:00. In fact, the following year, that is exactly what he did. Then he ran back to me—I was just beyond the halfway point—and he finished the race with me.

To this day, that race remains, for me, one of the most poignant real-life allegories of what it means for us to be Christ to one another.

Christ, the God-man, came down to earth and matched our pace, allowing us a glimpse of God.

Those guys and I didn't just physically run beside one another. We were spiritual running partners as well, and in that part of it, I was *their* pace-setter. We participated in mission trips together and more service projects and Bible studies than I can remember, along with other members of our church and youth group.

"As [the disciples] talked and discussed these things with each other [on the road to Emmaus], Jesus himself came up and walked along with them" (Luke 24:15).

Jesus materialized out of nowhere and walked beside these two disheartened disciples. And now, through the Holy Spirit, he does the same for us. Christ, the God-man, came down to earth and matched our pace, allowing us a glimpse of God.

Now we are to do the same for one another. You are not running this race alone. You have never been alone. My running partner is a carpenter. And he reveals himself to me through others who run this faith-race beside me.

Who are your faith-race running partners?

In what ways do they walk beside you?

What is one way that you can encourage/dare them?

Who can you encourage in the faith-race today?

Dare—Shoot a faith partner a message, using *at least* 20 words, thanking that person for a specific way he or she has encouraged you to grow in your faith.

Double Dare—Time yourself for one mile. Set a goal to achieve a mile within a certain time - walking, running, biking, treadmill, or even swimming. See if a friend or two would like to do the same with you.

Triple Dare—Sign up for that 5K or 10K you've been looking at with someone that you want to get to know better from your church or community. Extra points for dressing in silly costumes on race day.

Gorge Train and Encouraging Other Christians

Good things we do encourage others
Read Hebrews 6:9-12

There is a tourist train that runs through the 1,000-foot-deep Royal Gorge of the Arkansas River. The run follows the tracks laid down by the Denver-Rio Grande Railroad at the turn of the last century.

It's pretty cool.

And while it not only makes this place and all its beauty and scenery easily accessible to so many others, it also does this without a single additional impact to the environment itself. Grandparents that could never hop into a whitewater raft can view it all: the raging river, the sheer rock walls, the colorful geologic patterns. All from the comfort of a climate-controlled railcar with overhead windows offering unobstructed views of the wonders around them.

Every train through the Gorge also has its own version of "the cheap seats": an uncovered, unheated, wide-open railcar. Open to all the sounds and smells of the journey, as well as any chilly weather or precipitation, it offers complete and expansive views of the history and geology passing by, and one more thing...

During the 21-mile round-trip, should you happen to come across some brave groups running the river below, sometimes as few as 30 feet away, those in the open car can briefly interact with the rafters.

I've run plenty of people down that stretch of water and waving at the passenger train is always a regular event for my paddle crews. We point the boat, drop paddles, and wave at the kids, "woohoo" the adults, and toss "shakas" (Google it) at anyone pointing a phone or video camera. It was a blast for my crew and the train passengers always seemed to enjoy it as well.

Even better, the later it gets into the autumn season and the less traffic on the river, the more train passengers seem to appreciate it when a boat floats past.

Running a trip in late September, you not only get waves and smiles, but many times, also raucous cheers, clapping, and fist pumps in the air! The groups watching are more than just surprised to see you running alongside them down in that deep, dark gorge—they are positively thrilled by it!

To be able to bring such joy and crazy excitement to others, just by floating along, doing what you already happened to be doing. What a total blast! And also, a whole lot like how our Christian walk works.

Let us consider how we may spur one another on toward love and good deeds.
Hebrews 10:24

If seeing someone rafting a river can get people excited, what then is the impact of someone seeing you holding a door open for a woman with a baby stroller? Or shoveling snow from an older neighbor's driveway? Maybe you're tall and helped reach for someone's item on a store shelf. Simple, right? But then maybe someone saw you do it, and was spurred on to hug their spouse extra hard when they got home that night, and...

Our good deeds spur others on towards their own good deeds. Thank-you emails, "Atta boys" in front of the staff; the impact reverberates, everyone benefiting, everyone spurred into action towards those around them. And it can all start with us.

Lending a hand, giving recognition, letting someone else go first. There's no telling what good things will happen down the road as a direct result of your good deeds. Bonus—there's no telling how that same domino effect will draw the lost to Christ, simply by the actions you chose.

"Live such good lives among the pagans that, though they accuse you of doing wrong, they may see your good deeds and glorify God on the day he visits us" (1 Pet. 2:12).

Yup, potentially drawing people to Christ just by choosing patience in the parking lot after a school concert is what I read here. No kidding!

So go for it. Be creative, taking whatever opportunities present themselves, or asking God to specifically open your eyes to possibilities around you. Either way, have some fun today. Knowing that whether you see it or not, you're spurring others on all around you, and that somewhere along the line, someone lost could someday be praising our Lord God in heaven because of it.

Dare—Do one good deed today for someone that will not directly benefit you.

Double Dare—Choose two good deeds this morning, afternoon, and night. Do at least one without the other person's knowledge (use those ninja skills!).

Triple Dare—Choose to do "good deeds" this morning, afternoon, and night—all as listed above—but one each at home, work/school, and for a friend.

Optional "good deed idea starters"—

- Write your wife, kids, or friends postcards on your next business trip. The more exotic the better.
- Be the guy with the jumper cables.
- Hand off the remote to someone else for the entire night.
- Offer to drive everyone, in your car, the next three times it comes up.
- Find the person who never gets compliments about their appearance—find something to compliment.
- Pick up the tab at lunch with others.
- Buy the coffee for the person behind you in the drive thru.
- Buy the meal for the person behind you at a fast food drive thru.
- Let the other person choose the music in the car.
- Be the guy that offers a lift to a person in need of a ride.
- Let the other person take home the leftover pizza.
- Share your "toys" with someone else (day on the boat, waterskiing, wave-runner, quads, 4x4...).
- Big TV? Offer to host whatever TV parties come up the next three months.
- Big TV? Offer to host the next X-Box night.
- Big TV? Offer to host the next Bourne-movie marathon.

Lover's Leap of Faith

Adventure on the road less traveled
Read 2 Corinthians 4:7-18

We pressed back against the wall and walked cautiously along the four-foot-wide ledge, which became even narrower in some places. At one juncture, rain had washed the path away completely, leaving a one-foot gap. Four of us jumped across the gap on our own. Next, the two youngest kids—ages four and five—would need to be passed across the space.

Starved Rock State Park, in Illinois, derives its name from a legend in which one Indian tribe cornered and *starved* another tribe up on a ridge. There is also a cliff named Lover's Leap where, as legend recounts, a warrior of the one tribe fell in love with the princess from the other. Rather than being fated to live apart, they chose to die together—hence the cliff, Lover's Leap.

I have been to Starved Rock. I have been to Lover's Leap, too, but not like most people. There are paths—broad, defined, well-marked paths. Paths for Dummies, if you will. And yet.

My family and the friends we were hiking with managed to get off the beaten path. At first, we easily navigated the woods, but the path became as narrow as our options. Turning back never occurred to my father, not once. *That* is where I get it from.

We were not lost enough to be worried, but lost enough to say things like, "Well, that," upon spotting a railing, "looks like something." In order to reach this railing, we would have to climb a steep height of some 30 feet. The abundance of obvious footholds worked in our favor. However, between us and the base of the climb was a chasm—20 feet wide.

Fresh out of chickens and roads, nature provided only one way to get to the other side, in the form of a ledge that wrapped along a concave cliff face.

Logic would have turned around. Tenacity pressed forward.

We pressed our sides against the wall and inched along. We didn't talk much. Where rain had washed away the path completely, one of the adults jumped first. I and two others followed. Then my dad stretched out his arms and passed my youngest sister across the space into the waiting arms of the other adult.

Once we made it to the wider ground on the other side, those last steep 30 feet seemed simple. With inspiring team initiative, the seven of us climbed up toward the railing—the something.

Grateful to have survived, and excited to be finished with our adrenaline-packed adventure, I reached the dark brown wooden railing first. I climbed over the top and became the recipient of some very strange facial expressions.

My eyes bounced off their audacious stares to the plaque on the railing. Then the stares made sense.

Helping the others clamber over the railing, I shouted, "Hey, Dad, we just climbed up Lover's Leap!"

As he reached the top, my father shrugged and said to the families staring at us, "We like to keep things exciting."

See, while they were cautiously leaning over the railing, imagining a couple plummeting to their demise, seven people scaled the cliff to say hello. We were, quite literally, one step away from death. The climb was dangerous, difficult and frightening. And also, rewarding.

For our light and momentary troubles are achieving for us an eternal glory that far outweighs them all.
2 Corinthians 4:17

Who was more grateful for the view at the top?

The other families laughed as they hiked the broad path, five abreast, up to Lover's Leap. They snapped a few carefully-posed pictures with their cameras and read the information about the height of the cliff and the legend of the two lovers.

My family talked less and less as we climbed. We spoke only to encourage and spur one another on. We were too preoccupied with living to take pictures of living, and we didn't have to read a sign about the height of the cliff. We experienced it for ourselves.

Most visitors associate the glorious view from the top of the cliff with tragedy and death. But to us, Lover's Leap represented life. Life lived to the fullest, life experienced together, life accomplished in spite of difficulties. The adrenaline boost didn't hurt, either.

There is nothing conventional about following Christ. Known to the rest of the world as a symbol of death, to us, the cross portrays life. His call to follow pulls us away from the well-beaten path and beckons us to a place of great risk and high-adventure. Logic clashes with faith as we traverse through bushwhacked wilderness behind the Sword of the Spirit. But every so often, Jesus brings us to a something, a clearing, so that we can see in hindsight what he understood all along.

This is my will, he seems to say. *Isn't it beautiful?*

"So we fix our eyes not on what is seen, but on what is unseen, since what is seen is temporary, but what is unseen is eternal" (2 Cor. 4:18).

The cross is a symbol of death to the world, but to believers, the cross portrays life.

Dare—Find a spot outside where you can appreciate God's creation. Reflect there for 15 minutes.

Double Dare—Take the road less traveled. Find a simple path to explore, preferably late day or after work, and less than two hours.

Triple Dare—Mark your calendar to take a hike with friends or family. Make it a long enough distance that it requires you to pack a lunch. Include at least one fun item that will surprise your companions. Share it.

Three at the Top Equals Thirty in the Middle

Giving an answer for my hope
Read 1 Peter 3:8-16

When learning to be a whitewater guide, you do it mostly through on-the-job training. Mistakes are included for free, and lessons might include someone telling you, "Don't pump your boat tubes so hard next time and you might not flip." Others revolve around the more obvious, such as locating a source of bleeding and telling you to "be more careful."

Whether it's an obvious "you're doing it wrong," or a mundane "let me show you how," sometimes training insights go above and beyond, and become useful guidelines for years of river running to come.

One example: "Three strokes at the top equals thirty in the middle." This little gem was shared with me on one of my early wilderness river trips. These outings were far from the narrow, rock-strewn rivers back home in Colorado, and took us instead to large, swollen giants rolling through the deserts of the American West.

Cataract Canyon. Desolation Canyon. Westwater, and more. All legendary, all terrific examples of big-water rafting on high-volume rivers the width of football fields, and filled with re-circulating hydraulics the size of the house I grew up in.

When I dropped into these monsters, I learned the all-important lesson of setting up early. "Three strokes" in your setup would have you prepped for the entire run, simply hanging on and enjoying the ride. Miss them though, and you would spend "thirty strokes" or more trying to recover throughout the length of the rapid.

To miss your setup was to be that poor soul seen in so many YouTube videos, flailing bravely at the oars, moving merely a half-boat's width back towards center before dropping into some "boat-eating" cataclysm known as Satan's Gut, Crystal Hole, or The Room of Doom.

Have you ever found yourself flailing in the middle of something? A presentation? A persuasive sales pitch? Maybe a high-stakes exam, or something similar? "The well-prepared man need not fear," someone once said. He may well have been a Grand Canyon raft guide.

And if ever in our Christian life someone suddenly asked us, "Why *do* you believe what you say you believe?" Could we easily share an answer? Could we do it without flailing?

Peter not only assures us of our faith in Christ, but by this third chapter of his first letter to the early believers, he also encourages us to be ready to answer this very question of "why."

"...Always be prepared to give an answer to everyone who asks you to give the reason for the hope that you have" (1 Pet. 3:15).

What is the reason for my faith? Was it something I received going to church as a child? Does it revolve around an electrifying story of sudden, miraculous change in my life? Or did I simply find it reasonable to believe what the Bible asks me to believe?

But do this with gentleness and respect.
1 Peter 3:15

Whatever the case, we are also encouraged, nay, required by our high-energy brother-in-Christ, Peter, to convey this answer with the utmost respect and humility. Always. No trying to outdo someone's arguments against Christ. No notches in our belt for shutting down a non-believer. Rather, we are to be servants of the light Christ has entrusted to us, not "burning" others in our zeal to share it.

Take a moment and answer Peter's question for yourself. Why *do* you believe what you say you believe? Share your answer out loud with the cats, the dashboard, or the houseplants. Does it sound forced or natural? Does it flow? Is it humble and respectful in the way that you share it?

If it could use some work, you're not alone. Worst case, come up with a 30-second pitch for why you follow Christ. For example, "The Bible says that following Christ offers freedom, joy, peace, and purpose. Why wouldn't I want that?" From there, have a handle on the bullet points of the reasons for your faith, i.e. my parents raised me in the church, I wanted more from life, following Christ has made me a better husband, father, co-worker, boss, etc...

Whatever answer you arrive at, no matter how short, silly, boring, or mundane-sounding, fear not, for you have just officially taken your "three strokes at the top" in preparing to give an answer for the hope you have in Christ.

Now go have some fun answering others' questions confidently and with grace, knowing that whatever comes along, you will no longer be some guy flailing wildly in the middle of a bunch of furious whitewater.

====

Why do you believe what you say you believe?

====

Dare—The most obvious one yet… Out loud, give your answer to the question, "Why do you believe what you say you believe?"

Double Dare—Give your answer, then share it with your wife or trusted friend. (The cat does not count.)

Triple Dare—Give your answer, then share it with a group of others— Bible study, men's group, fellow believers on movie night. Afterwards, encourage each one of them to give it a try. Encourage any that "flail" with what you've just read. Be their hero.

The Devil's Punch Bowl

Churning the heart
Read Jonah 1:1-15

A fierce wind whipped off the Pacific. With each step, our gym shoes sank into the sand as the three of us walked along the shore.

It was dusk and high tide as we made our way back up the beach and to the stairs that would lead us to the car.

A rapid *chop-chop-chop* caught our attention and we turned toward the sound. An orange-and-white Coast Guard helicopter zipped up the shoreline, approaching from the south, flying right over us. The waves scattered, pushed back with the force of the rotating blades.

Our eyes followed the helo as it approached a high cliff face that jutted upward at the water's edge, where we could see a man and a woman standing helpless on a ledge. Their silhouettes were barely visible against the violet sky. The rocks they had ascended were submerged by the tide. Now, angry waves licked at their perch, blocking their escape.

"How did they miss the rising tide?" I wondered—and, yes, I admit, indignantly.

I wouldn't get trapped like that.

"Maybe they slipped down from up above by the Devil's Punch Bowl," my friend concluded. "And then they couldn't get back up *or* climb down."

"The Devil's Punch Bowl?" our other friend asked.

"We'll show it to you," we promised.

The three of us fell silent and watched as a Coast Guard member was lowered from the helicopter. He swung a harness over to each person and, one at a time, the rope hoisted them into the safety of the helicopter.

"The Devil's Punch Bowl isn't far—well, relatively speaking," I added as we approached the steps that led to the top of the cliff.

The Devil's Punch Bowl is a hollowed-out rock formation about 30 yards in diameter. Water comes in through an opening at the bottom and the waves crashing inside cause the water to churn, giving it a cauldron, or punch bowl, appearance. The red-and-brown walls are high and slick, which makes them nearly impossible to climb. I've never seen anyone in the Punch Bowl. It's fenced off, and motivated hikers have to circle around the cove or rappel into the ocean in order to get to the narrow opening at its base—an opening which is submerged in water, except at low tide.

We watched as the water churned, constantly colliding with itself, a contained fury.

For a person to be in the Punch Bowl at low tide would be dangerous. At high tide, with waves whipping from one side of the rock wall to the other, it would prove fatal.

The three of us leaned over the fence and watched as the water churned, constantly colliding with itself, a contained fury.

"But Jonah had gone below deck, where he lay down and fell into a deep sleep. The captain went to him and said, 'How can you sleep? Get up and call on your god! Maybe he will take notice of us so that we will not perish'" (Jonah 1:5-6).

Jonah slept. There was a storm wreaking havoc in Jonah's world—Assyrians stranded and steeped in their own sin; the men ferrying Jonah while also fighting for their lives—and still he slept.

Jonah slept through God's call on his life and was indifferent to the love God had for his people. It took a violent, God-sized storm to churn Jonah into action. Even then, Jonah obeyed God with a hard heart, not a broken one. And Jonah's sole display of passion for God's compassion was anger, not desperation or love.

Are you sleep-walking through the broken world around you? Have you known of someone in need of God's compassion and simply turned the other way?

Parents in the throes of alcohol and drug addiction. A teen headed down a destructive path. Human trafficking. People who have never experienced the love of God. Does your heart break for those God's heart breaks for—his children in need of rescue? What will you let God do about it through you?

The people in our communities who are the hardest to love, the ones we often judge, are the same people who need our love the most. If God called you to love your enemy, or at the very least, the needy and unlovable people in your life, where would you start?

Dare—Pray for Christians in foreign countries. When getting dressed each morning, look at your clothing label and pray for the churches in the "made in" nation. Shirt = Christians in Singapore, tie = China, etc.

Double Dare—Pray for those you don't know. Your future wife, your son's future wife, your future son-in-law... They're all out there. Pray for their safety and happiness throughout today, ideally, or anytime you stop to eat.

Triple Dare—Pray for something long-term. A friend or family member coming to Christ maybe? Put it somewhere visible (bathroom mirror, desk) where you'll see it frequently. Now, get up before dawn one day in the next two weeks, just to pray for this specific thing. Preferably near a window.

Living Your Purpose

I love this photo.

Sure, the elements all work well—backlit water spray, sun just out of frame, offset subject—but what I really love is the expression captured on the girl's face. Tightly-squeezed eyes, head turning from the wave, and that barely visible smile of pure joy. You can almost hear her squeal. I love it.

I pulled the photo out of some video that I shot on a late-season rafting trip last year.

I like to rig one of those rugged, waterproof cameras in my boat sometimes. You know, to catch fun video of our boats running rapids, or even better, people getting tossed around, boats flipping... Whatever.

There was no carnage, unfortunately, but the camera still rolled the whole time and we all had a blast.

Back home, as I looked through the footage, it appeared to be pretty boring with nothing really worth pulling out and sharing, until I happened across this one brief instant. I paused the video, rewound, and moved through the clip frame-by-frame, until I saw this one particular moment from that day. Just 1/60th of a second long, I grabbed it.

Now, the thing to realize about this specific screen capture is that it was picked out of two hours of footage, captured at 60 frames per second. That's right, the camera recorded 60 images, every second, for our entire two-hour run down the river.

If I do the quick math, that's approximately 432,000 images, with this lone frame being the only one that I liked well enough to pull out. Seems like an awful lot of wasted video, no?

And if my perspective is to look at that video as two hours of film with just one single good frame, then that would certainly be true.

But what if, instead, I look at that delightful portrait, that hidden gem, as the entire reason for the shooting of the video at all. Suddenly, the rest of the film isn't a waste, but becomes the necessary effort that made that one single image even possible.

A mountain of boring video images that leads up to and gives us a single moment that is absolutely beautiful and that we can't wait to share with others.

Any chance this reminds you of your current season in life?

Ever feel like you're doing all the right things, but there just doesn't appear to be any real impact?

Are you working away, confident that you're following God's path, but not seeing anything "worth pulling out and sharing" in your day-to-day? Why is it that sometimes it seems like we're in the right place, doing all the right things, but there just doesn't appear to be any real impact?

Sometimes fulfilling our purpose doesn't feel all that purposeful.

It reminds me of Abraham, one of the all-time masters of steadily following God, despite only glimpsing the impact his faithful serving would have in the millennia to come. Sure, Abraham had God's promise to trust in, but then again, so do we. Even more so!

So how will God use the time and effort you've been pouring into something recently? The work project you've given so much of your life to. Those networks and relationships you've steadily invested your heart and soul into. The times you've volunteered your energy and skills, only to see, seemingly, no result.

Can we trust that, just as one single fun image might be found amidst hours of mediocre video, how much more so our heavenly Father has woven his amazing purposes into your efforts, no matter how mundane or ordinary they seem?

Don't give up.

I found a beautiful photo. God made Abraham the father of a nation. What will God surprise you with as a result of your continued hard work and faithfulness in this time?

"Let us not become weary in doing good, for at the proper time we will reap a harvest if we do not give up" (Gal. 6:9).

Dare—Pause and appreciate all you have around you, right now. Friends, family, loved ones, job, home, health… Even if life is in a bit of a dry spell, take a moment to let God know you appreciate it, and thank him for it.

Double Dare—Revisit how God has used you in the past. Remember his promises. Have any sin in your life? Deal with it. Listening for God? Perfect. Know that God has plans for you (Jer. 29:11) and that as long as you're not running off like Jonah, everything you do today (Rom. 8:28) is moving you along the path God has for you.

Triple Dare—Connect the dots on where you've been, and where you currently are. Any chance it reveals the direction things are moving in, even if not immediately apparent? Moses, too, experienced a lull (Ex. 2:22-23), which God utilized to train Moses for the rest of his story. How might God be doing the very same for you in your current circumstances?

Prayer Winks

God's sense of humor
Read Acts 12:1-17

I watched them climb up the exact same bluff from which the Coast Guard had recently rescued another couple.

This could end badly.

Then I followed. I hadn't seen my sister or brother-in-law for more than two years, and this was their one chance to see the coast. Not only that, but how could we pass up such a perfect, humorous answer to prayer?

Rewind several hours.

"Our" spot along the coast wasn't too far out of the way on our drive from the airport to my house. But only about ten minutes or so from our destination, the windshield wipers whipped back and forth at the highest speed.

I parked the car, staring at the sheet of rain that streamed down the windows, fighting back my disappointment. I listened to them debate whether or not getting out to see the view was worth getting drenched.

"God, is there any way that you can hold off the rain while we're here? This is the only time we could come." I stated this to him as if he didn't already know it. "Please? Just hit 'pause' and then you can start the rain up again as soon as we're finished."

"Amen," we said in unison. The rain didn't miraculously stop.

"How long should we give him?" I asked.

"Five minutes," my brother-in-law answered. And just five minutes later, the downpour relented to a drizzle. Sometimes answers to prayer come with some faith assembly required.

We got out of the car and headed down the stairs from the bluff. As we neared the beach at the bottom, the rain stopped. Slate gray clouds still threatened an encore, but God held the rain at bay.

The waves slid up almost to our shoes as we meandered toward the cove, where months earlier, a couple trapped by the rising tide had been rescued by the Coast Guard. I didn't mention that nugget of information to my sister and her husband. They're more cautious then I am, and the announcement would have sent them scrambling back down at break-neck speed. As we clambered up the rocky bluff, I cautiously eyed the waves tipping over boulders at the base.

We stayed up there for some time. Every so often, I'd look down and check the tide. When strong waves shattered against the rocks, I nonchalantly suggested it was time to return to the main beach. Safe on dry sand, I finally told them about the Coast Guard rescue.

They both stopped and stared at me. "You might have mentioned that."

"I just did."

An hour later we were ready to leave, and in all that time it hadn't rained. But as I stepped on the first wooden stair at the edge of the beach, I noticed that it was speckled with fat round drops.

God stayed the rain until the moment that we left, just like we had asked. Coincidence?

We thanked God, and as we ascended the steps, the rain began falling harder. By the time we reached the top, we were bolting to the car.

God stayed the rain, just as we asked. Coincidence?

Sometimes God reveals his sense of humor to us through our prayers.

"So Peter was kept in prison, but the church was earnestly praying to God for him.

"The night before Herod was to bring him to trial, Peter was sleeping between two soldiers, bound with two chains, and sentries stood guard at the entrance.

"Suddenly an angel of the Lord appeared... and struck Peter on the side and woke him up. 'Quick, get up!' he said, and the chains fell off Peter's wrists.

"Then the angel said to him, 'Put on your clothes and sandals.' And Peter did so. 'Wrap your cloak around you and follow me,' the angel told him" (Acts 12:5-7).

Peter followed the angel out of the prison, but thought he was dreaming!

"They passed the first and second guards and came to the iron gate leading to the city. It opened for them by itself, and they went through it. When they had walked the length of one street, suddenly the angel left him" (Acts 12:10).

When Peter realized he wasn't dreaming, he wnt to his friends' home —where people gathered to pray for him.

"Peter knocked at the outer entrance, and a servant named Rhoda came to answer the door.

"When she recognized Peter's voice, she was so overjoyed she ran back without opening it and exclaimed, 'Peter is at the door!'

"'You're out of your mind,' they told her. But Peter kept on knocking, and when they opened the door and saw him, they were astonished...Peter motioned with his hand for them to be quiet and described how the Lord had brought him out of prison" (Acts 12:13-17).

First, the angel gave Peter a good shove. Peter thought he was dreaming. His friends thought the servant was nuts, and the servant left a befuddled Peter knocking at the door while his friends prayed for his release! God had to have been dying of laughter as he watched that one play out.

Sometimes God reveals his sense of humor to us through our prayers.

My family's prayer to hold back the rain for a couple hours was not earth-shattering. But I believe that God was laughing when he answered it. That moment on the coast has become a personal joke, a prayer wink, between my Savior and me.

Despite the threatening rainstorm, it was all okay, because we'd asked our Lord God to hold back the rain just for us and I trusted that he would.

Dare—Today, pray and ask God for something specific, yet seemingly insignificant. Then, in faith, brace yourself for God's sense of humor.

Double Dare—Ask the question of church members during a fellowship time, "When was a time that God answered a specific prayer for you in a completely unexpected way?"

Triple Dare—Start a prayer journal or list to keep track of the way God answers your specific prayers. Re-visit it every month. What patterns do you see in your requests? In God's answers?

Seven Bad Decisions

One thing leads to another
Read James 1:2-16

T here's a theory in the rescue communities that any serious event is often the result of multiple poor decisions made beforehand. Had any one of them been made differently, it could have easily prevented a tragic outcome. This theory is sometimes referred to as the Seven Bad Decisions, and here's how it works:

You're planning to go late-season rafting with friends on a nearby river. You hit the snooze on your alarm one too many times and are running late (#1). You grab a chocolate bar, fill your water bottle, and dash off.

You arrive at the river, only to see clouds building upstream. In your hurry this morning, you forgot to check the weather forecast (#2). As shuttle vehicles pull away and head downstream, you check for your splash top, but realize you hung it up to dry last weekend…back in your garage. Any backup clothing is in your gear bag, which sits in one of the cars that just drove off. The breeze feels cool and you have no layers (#3).

You decide to enjoy the day despite conditions. Things go well for the first hour, and people are having fun. Splashing waves leave you chilled, but you'll muscle through and be fine. As you pull out for lunch, you find a spot in the sun. You're definitely cold, but the sun feels wonderful. Around you, others eat sandwiches and drink warm tea from their thermoses. You sip your water and have only the candy bar you brought (#4).

As people get ready to head back on the water, you're thinking of staying off and driving a shuttle vehicle instead. When you ask, someone says sorry, but they ran all the vehicles to the take-out this morning, and there's nothing parked at the halfway lunch spot. No vehicles to sit in and get warm, no possibility of scavenging someone else's warm layers, and no option to stay off this afternoon (#5). You will have to get back in a boat and finish the trip.

Within minutes you hit the first waves and are once again soaked. The warmth of the lunchtime sun is quickly fading, and you now need to paddle to keep from shivering. Still, it's less than an hour more and you can make it.

It is at this moment that "the incident" occurs.

It doesn't appear to be a big deal. A boat bumps a rock and one of the paddlers falls into the water. Except it's someone's girlfriend and her first time rafting. Also, nobody told her what to do if she fell out (#6), and she's rapidly being swept downstream. Every decision you have made up until this point is now going to either help you or hinder you in what comes next.

Your boat is just downstream and the current will carry her right past you. You could easily reach out to her with a paddle, but you're cold and not thinking clearly. Instead, you react by extending your hand, quickly realizing that you cannot possibly reach her. Clumsily you leave your arm outstretched and begin shouting at her to swim to you, but she sweeps past, only inches away. Time seems to slow as you watch her disappear into the rapid below. In the back of your mind, you hear someone's rescue whistle blowing.

Decision #7 has come and gone. The event is over; there are now only consequences.

From this example, it's clear that even an easy, routine situation can be greatly affected by the choices you make, both good and bad, prior to it. Sometimes hours or minutes before; other times only seconds.

Every decision you have made up until this point is now going to either help you, or hinder you, in what comes next.

Turning our eyes to the decision paths we read about in Scripture, there are similar patterns for our decisions in everyday life. Choices we make build upon each other like compounding interest and either make life easier or oh, so much harder.

One of these describes the step-by-step process of falling for sexual temptation: "…but each person is tempted when they are dragged away by their own evil desire and enticed. Then, after desire has conceived, it gives birth to sin; and sin, when it is full-grown, gives birth to death" (James 1:14-15).

It's just a harmless website link, right? Wow, that certainly is a low-cut shirt she's wearing. You're married, sure, but did she just smile at you?!? The list of everyday enticements in our culture goes on and on.

The good news? At any stage along this path, a single godly decision can short-circuit the entire process and point you to escape. Get out early enough and there will be little or no harm to you or others. Allow yourself to get sucked in, however, and you are heading for disaster; spiritual death and destroyed relationships are just a few of the consequences littering the path ahead of you.

Thankfully there's an equally clear path that we can walk, one decision at a time that, instead of death, leads towards something glorious! James touched on this early in our reading today but have a look as Paul unpacks this same process in his letter to the Romans.

"...but we also glory in our sufferings, because we know that suffering produces perseverance; perseverance, character; and character, hope" (Rom. 5:3-4).

So, choosing to stick it out in hard times brings perseverance, which leads to improved character, and that, according to James, results in our being "mature and complete, not lacking anything."

No bailing out, then. No choosing the path of least resistance. Each day, in every situation, over and over again, perseverance. The result? A glorious process automatically kicks in and works its magic, building our character, and inevitably leading us to a place where we lack for absolutely nothing.

Who says seven decisions always lead to something bad? Not if we choose wisely, my friends.*

================

Dare—Think of a time you fell for something dumb. And wrong. Some silly enticement to sit through a movie's sex scene or click a web link. Now, have some fun and track-back through the specific events leading up to that bad decision. Assess and identify—Where did it get out of your control? When could you have interrupted the cycle? Commit to doing so next time.

Double Dare—Nobody on a diet ever goes into a donut shop. Not if they value their diet. Do you and I value our reputations? Assess if you are allowing enticements into your life, anywhere, big or small, without meaning to.

Triple Dare—Think of an area in life where you see a real temptation to bail out (thankless work tasks, one-sided relationships, tough time lately with your wife...) Think through the specific, even brutal, consequences of persevering vs. bailing. Trusted employee vs. not at all. Modeling Christ vs. embarrassment to your kids. People looking up to you vs. people avoiding you. Yikes, the clear path is easy to see, right? Stand firm, baby!

---

*No hypothetical persons were harmed in the imaginative writing of this Devotion.

Look Down

Pride vs. humility
Read Obadiah. The *entire* book. I dare you.

Fear paralyzed me. Then I heard my name and he gripped my wrist.

Some college friends and I had decided to take a walk in Estes Park, Colorado. We carried no ropes, no harnesses, no carabiners. We didn't need them for a *walk*. But the walk turned into a hike and the hike turned into a climb.

The wide dirt path narrowed, wrapping itself around the birches and evergreens that towered above us, sheltering us in a canopy of limbs, leaves and needles. The grade grew steeper. Dead twigs snapped beneath our gym shoes and patches of snow appeared, covering the low foliage on either side of us.

Hiking became hoisting and the handholds fewer and farther between. The footholds of real estate seemed to be shrinking, too. I was more worried, though, about looking stupid in front of my friends—who seemed to be climbing without a problem—than I was scared. We came to one particular outcrop, essentially vertical. Three others started climbing ahead of me. Pride propelled my body forward and upward, as my mind flashed neon signs of *Warning* and *Danger*. Two friends decided to stay put. They'd reached their limit and were not embarrassed to admit it.

Then I looked to the left—don't look down—and was startled by my proximity to, well, death. Hundreds of feet down, the river we'd crossed earlier looked like a narrow ribbon snaking through the evergreens. I pancaked my body to the vertical rock wall, heels hanging off the narrow lip that I was perched upon.

I forgot to care about what my friends thought. I slowly turned my head back to the rock in front of me, afraid that if I moved too quickly I would lose my footing and fall. My lips brushed against the cold rock, my clammy palms flattened against the escarpment. I feared even the slight inflating of my chest as I inhaled. I hesitate to admit this, but I may have actually whimpered.

"Sam." My friend, secure on the ledge above, reached down toward me. His hand clamped around my wrist. "Left foot thigh-high."

I exhaled in a shaky breath and placed my left foot on the tiny, thigh-high hold.

"One," he said.

"Two. Three," we said together.

I shoved myself upward as he pulled. My right foot found another perch and seconds later I stood on a broad surface with my friends. The hammering pulse in my ears faded away and I marveled at the timberline visible on the snow-dusted peaks across the canyon. The river of cobalt ribbon threaded its way downstream, throwing off fire as ripples reflected the light of the late afternoon sun.

Do you struggle with pride? Has it ever inhibited you or negatively affected your self-esteem or your relationships with others?

The Christian life, lived through Christ's example of leaving heaven for earth, and trading prosperity for sacrifice, is a life of humility.

Humble yourselves before the Lord and he will lift you up in due time.

James 4:10

Humility says *I can't do this by myself.* Humility has no spare change for condescending thoughts about others. In humility, we understand that *anything* good about ourselves comes from God.

Pride was the downfall of the Edomites. The Edom-who-hites? The Edomites, descendants of Esau, the brother of Jacob (Israel). Edom, a mountainous nation, used to lie to the southeast of Canaan, the Promised Land, now Israel. High, craggy red rock provided natural fortification for Petra, Edom's capital city. A person could only enter into Petra through one narrow opening on the ground. (Sorta like a *really big* Devil's Punch Bowl.) The Edomites haughtily looked down on Israel. Their pride stemmed from their belief that Petra would hold against any enemy.

And their arrogance outweighed their compassion. When Israel fled from Egypt, Edom denied Israel a safe and peaceful passage through the main highway. With Edom's show of military force, the Israelites had no choice but to circumvent Edom and travel through the desert.

The entire book of Obadiah (okay, so it's only 21 verses) describes in detail Edom's sins against Judah during Babylon's siege. Edom stood aloof while strangers carried off Judah's wealth; they gloated and rejoiced at the Israelites' misfortune and cut down fugitives at the crossroads, handing the survivors over to the Babylonians. God, furious with their condescending treatment of his people, said, *"There will be no survivors from Esau"* (Ob. 18). And there aren't. The country of Jordan now exists where the descendants of Esau once did. Pride comes before the fall.

In my case, being left behind while the others ascended was unthinkable! Sense of adventure, yes, but the greater determinant was pride. I refused to be out-climbed. Can you relate?

For all I knew, the two people at the bottom had remained there. Yet, when I finally reached the top, there they stood. I looked at one of them quizzically. "Oh," he pointed over his shoulder. "We found a path on the other side."

Nice. Humble yourself before the Lord and he will lift you up in due time.

Has pride ever made your life more difficult or prevented you from helping someone in need?

Be careful of having thoughts like, *he deserved it* or *what goes around comes around. She had it coming.* These statements run in direct opposition to the purity of heart that God desires.

Humility is knowing that anything good in us is from God.

Dare—Pick one specific prayer request related to humility and pray over it daily for one week. Examine how it changed (if at all) over the week (i.e. bless my friend—no, bless my friend with wisdom—no, bless him with wisdom concerning this job choice).

Double Dare—Pick one specific prayer request and pray over it daily for ten days. Examine how it changed (if at all) over this time.

Triple Dare—What's that thing that you've always wanted to learn, but you've been afraid to admit you don't already know? (Grilling? Fishing? Rules of Hockey?) Find someone who can teach you *and* schedule a specific day and time to get together.

Throw Ropes and Not Being Tied Down

Our stuff doesn't own us—right?
Read 1 Timothy 6:6-19

Ask commercial whitewater guides what they most count on from their boats in a pinch, and you might expect an answer like strong paddlers, or the med kit. Maybe their guide paddle. All good answers, but for me, in the event of a river emergency, I'd grab my throw bag first.

An orange nylon bag about the size of a football, filled with 75 feet of bright yellow, floating polypropylene line attached at the bottom. You could toss it to a swimmer, tie off a boat to shore, rig a clothesline for wet layers, or in the event of a pinned raft, create a simple 3:1 mechanical advantage rescue-rope system.

Yup, rafting guides definitely love their throw bags.

There is nothing more satisfying than watching a quick, dynamic toss of your bag sail out over the water, touchdown-pass style, trailing coils of rope behind it, then slowly dropping and landing with a splash just over the shoulder of your swimmer. As they grab the line draped across their chest, you simply hold them tight as they drift through a wide arc, right back to shore, and to safety. Ahhhh…

The only caveat when "bagging swimmers"? Instruct them to never, ever wrap the rope around their hand. Or their wrist. Because unlike the slick, plastic-braided rope found at home stores, this is serious, high-strength, dynamic rope protected by a nylon sheath, offering all the grip you'll need when holding on tight.

But if grabbing the rope feels secure, then one wrap around the wrist should be even more secure, right?

No doubt. In fact, it's potentially a little *too* secure…

Here's why. As you grab the rope lying across your chest, you'll continue to float downstream another few seconds before the rope becomes

119

taut. Feeling a slight jerk, your rescuer, just upstream, will hold the rope tight, allowing the river current to "pendulum" you back towards shore.

Should your rope happen to snag on a rock, you simply let go, and a second rescuer will "throw bag" you further down. Easy. And if the water's not too cold, it's even kind of fun.

Unless of course, you let go...but the rope doesn't.

Because once on tension, that rope you wrapped around your wrist will create a tremendous amount of friction against your skin and can wrap even tighter, not slipping off and away as you'd expected.

The impact to you?

Rather than swinging into shore, you're now stuck in the middle of a raging river, snagged on an obstruction you can't even see. Your wrist immediately becomes the focal point of the force of the water pushing against your body. Pain is a certainty, fractures likely.

Trapped mid-river in significant flows, water will rush over your head. Suffice to say, nobody wants to be "attached" to a rope in the middle of a river, unable to free themselves. Ever.

Is there anything in your life that has you feeling tied down, unable to free yourself? We're not talking about your work or family here, but something else. Something you invited in. Something that's now taken hold.

Does anything in your life have you feeling tied down, unable to free yourself?

Cool truck, but wow does it guzzle gas? Or, no room to park the second car in the garage because of all the stuff? Still shaking your head at a great deal on some gigantic, sub-prime mortgage home that you're still trying to repair your credit over?

"'Go, sell everything you have and give to the poor, and you will have treasure in heaven. Then come, follow me.' At this the man's face fell. He went away sad, because he had great wealth. Jesus looked around and said to his disciples, 'How hard it is for the rich to enter the kingdom of God'" (Mark 10:21-23).

Even Jesus saw how a person's possessions could hold him hostage. Imagine being called by Jesus himself, and then being either unwilling, or unable, to respond, all because of your stuff. Hard to believe, but have we ever allowed it to happen to us?

Is it a schedule bursting with plans and meetings every single night of the week? Hey, can you help us this week? Nope, booked. Can we count on you? Sorry, already have something going that night.

Promised your kids a weekend camping trip, but then remembered a prior work commitment? Maybe you'd love to attend that marriage weekend in the mountains, but you're still working off some credit card debt.

Rescue ropes are fine things, but only when used properly, thus preventing them from causing harm. Similarly, let's make sure our possessions or schedules—perfectly fine when kept in check —are never permitted to control our lives, or to get in the way of our pursuing and responding to the things that God wants our attention on.

The things we know we should absolutely be pursuing.

Dare—Recall anything in your life that has ever caused you to say "no" to something you felt led by God to do? When was the last time you remember possessions getting in the way of something/anything fun, healthy, or good for your marriage?

Double Dare—Take an opportunity in the next seven days to gather up anything you've been meaning to give away. Simple test—if you moved tomorrow, would you care if this thing was ever unpacked at the new location? If not, toss it in a box and donate it to a local non-profit. Nice work.

Triple Dare—Do a quick inventory of your possessions. Donate one box from the garage or basement, one from a closet (you choose). Toss outdated paperwork. Delete or archive emails and old computer files. Take a quick walk-thru video of everything else in case of an insurance claim due to fire.

A Spry 93

As I traipsed through the woods with two gentlemen from church, I presumed to think, regarding one of them, *this man is 110 years old. I'll have no trouble keeping up.* Okay, not really 110, only 93 —but still.

Even so, our elderly guide took off through the trees at a pace that astonished my friend and me, and we hastened our steps to keep up. This spry little guy vaulted over large fallen trees. My efforts felt like clumsy blundering in comparison.

He blazed his own trail through the forest.

However, it soon became evident that he was lost. Whatever he was bent on showing us had not magically manifested itself where he expected it to.

He began muttering to himself, oblivious to my friend and me, who exchanged questioning looks. As the possibility that we'd be out past nightfall sank in, my friend drew his cell phone from his pocket and checked for service. No dice. We watched as our tour guide turned in a circle, taking in his surroundings.

Then our elderly companion did something that I will never forget. He paused in a small clearing, looked at his watch and then at the sky. He double-checked his math, located the moss growing on a nearby tree, and without any further hesitation darted off once again through the woods. My friend and I had another silent conversation, then continued in hot pursuit.

Moss grows on the north side of a tree. And in case you missed it, Davy Crockett was able to calculate course direction using the time of day and the sun's position in the sky.

Can you do that? I can't. Once, two friends and I were out joyriding. I was daydreaming in the backseat when they interrupted to ask me where we were and how to get home. They couldn't even tell me what direction we were going.

"Alright," I said, as we came upon a major highway. All highways that run north to south are odd-numbered, and all even-numbered highways run east to west. "We are either going north or south. Keep driving." When we got to the next highway, I knew that we were heading north. "Turn right to go home," I said. That was easy—navigating with roads and signs and well-assigned numbers.

Finding my way through a forest using the position of the sun in the sky—yeah, not going to happen.

But for my 93-year-old Davy Crockett, the sun and the moss might as well have been reflective highway signs.

This time, with this remarkable man's guidance, we came upon the path that he'd expected to find. It was as narrow as a deer trail, and I still couldn't help doubting. I tried to tell myself that it looked more promising than the forest we'd been climbing through, but that didn't work. Until.

In the middle of the woods, in the middle of nowhere, was a crude, rugged old cross.

The forest gave way to a clearing, and in the middle of the woods, in the middle of nowhere, was a crude, rugged old cross with log benches leading up to it. He'd led us to an outdoor chapel.

The inexplicable peace of God's presence replaced every cynical thought. With some sort of silent agreement that words would destroy the moment, we each chose our own bench and paused for several minutes of reflection.

"'And you, my child, will be called a prophet of the Most High; for you will go on before the Lord to prepare the way for him, to give his people the knowledge of salvation through the forgiveness of their sins, because of the tender mercy of our God, by which the rising sun will come to us from heaven to shine on those living in darkness and in the shadow of death, to guide our feet into the path of peace'" (Luke 1:76-79).

This is what the priest Zechariah said of his son—John the Baptist. John paved the way for Jesus. Jesus paved the way for us.

Jesus' presence on earth was pivotal for the Jewish people. Even the Roman calendar (though several years off) revolves around the birth of Christ. Before Jesus, the Israelites wandered through a self-constructed forest, guided by an outdated perception of the Messiah. And just as the star over Bethlehem pointed the shepherds and wise men to the true Messiah, Jesus—the Light of the World—guided the Israelites and the rest of the world to the truth of who God is.

I can almost see Jesus shaking the scrolls that the religious leaders' noses were buried in and shouting, "Look at me! Don't you get it? These prophecies are pointing to me!" The Messiah they waited so desperately for stood right in front of them, desiring to share his heart with them. And they missed it. They were so close to the truth, and yet they couldn't see it.

We are no different. But the scrolls that we have our noses buried in are electronic and palm-sized with swipe screens. Our self-constructed forests are jam-packed with to-do lists dictated to us by electronic Roman calendars. Busyness sprouts up all around us and prevents us from finding peace in the presence of that old rugged cross.

Your Messiah is walking close by and he desires to share his ideas with you. Are you missing it?

Dare—Don't turn on the radio in your car during your commute or just running around, until you've prayed first. Be sure to include: Praising God for who he is, sharing something you're struggling with, thanking God for something he's done or provided, and asking for your needs and others'.

Double Dare—Commit to praying a 10-second prayer, thanking God and for one specific thing, every time you stop to eat something.

Triple Dare—Embark on a word fast. No speaking for 1, 4, 8, 12, or even 24 hours. You'll be amazed at what God can reveal to you.

Perspective on God

Ignorance is bliss, but what else?
Read Philippians 4:4-9

There I was, perched on a thin ledge at the very edge of a 35-foot drop, legs dangling out into space, and feeling…nothing. Fear? Nope. Nervousness? Not at all. Anxiety? Oddly enough, even leaning out and looking down past my knees, trying to summon a tiny bit of worry, made no difference. It simply wasn't there.

Why? Because I was climbing in a pitch-black cave.

Now, I'm not a huge fan of spelunking, or crawling around in caves, but when I got an invite to join some friends, really, how could I say no? The day outside was lovely, but that ceased to matter the moment we squirmed through a narrow culvert into Manitou Cave. Luckily Manitou is a dry cave, so there were no worries about getting cold and wet, but we anticipated some tight squeezes. And so with headlamps on and knee pads at the ready, we wriggled in.

We spent the next hour getting ridiculously dirty and learning valuable lessons, such as the widest part of your body is across your shoulders, and you always want a second, third, and even fourth backup light in a cave. Soon, however, we came to a facet in the ceiling called The Corkscrew. This cylindrical opening went almost straight up (about 35 feet according to the folks I was with) and was so named because there were outcrops every two to three feet along the sides. By spiraling around and bracing across the opening as you went up—not unlike a corkscrew—you could make your way quite far up into this narrow, vertical passage.

Oh, yes, please.

My progress was slow and steady, but regardless of any height I gained, it was nice to explore a feature that didn't require fully exhaling or contorting my tall frame to squeeze through yet another tight space. The freedom to stretch out my legs, even across a black, yawning abyss that plummeted straight down to the cave floor below, was actually refreshing.

127

And so I climbed, never aware of anything outside of the tiny sphere of light that my headlamp provided around me. I could have been five feet off the ground, or I could have been 25. I climbed on, eventually reaching the top of the passage and stopping to rest.

The view was just as limited, but I now knew I was at least 35 feet up. I thought of a friend who considered this to be his least favorite height when climbing—high enough to get badly hurt if you fell, but low enough that you'd still likely survive. I was in full agreement with him on this.

And yet…I felt nothing. Despite the obvious jeopardy, I was without fear. Why? Because I literally couldn't see any danger.

I would say this was almost too unreal to believe, but there I was, experiencing it for myself. And I'm not the only one. Our brothers in Christ described this very thing, a complete lack of fear despite their circumstances, long before my caving excursion.

Is it possible to have serenity while in full view of your precarious life situations?

David shared in the famous 23rd Psalm, "Even though I walk through the darkest valley, I will fear no evil, for you are with me….You prepare a table before me in the presence of my enemies" (Ps. 23:4, 5).

The Old Testament prophet Habakkuk, envisioning the ruin that was soon to come upon Jerusalem from the Babylonians, wrote, "I heard and my heart pounded, my lips quivered at the sound…Yet I will wait patiently for the day of calamity to come on the nation invading us" (Hab. 3:16).

And even Habakkuk is not alone finding peace despite his heart-pounding situation. In the letter Paul writes to his friends in Philippi, he describes a "peace that passes all understanding" (Phil. 4:7). A few verses later he records the ever popular "I have learned to be content in all circumstances" (Phil. 4:11). And the crazy thing was? Paul wrote that letter to the Philippians from a dark, dank prison cell. Sorta like a cave.

Ignorance might be a source of peace, I'll admit, but what I'm suggesting is, despite the precarious life situations we may find ourselves in, is it still possible to have serenity while in full view of them?

David, Paul, and Habakkuk each had a particular view of God that obviously changed the way they lived their lives and responded to their situations. David goes so far as to consider his own hair-raising circumstances as a perfectly good time to order a pizza.

In the midst of any craziness, we can breathe easy. Our sovereign Lord God has it all under control.

The idea is that you and I can relax while under fire. Simply because we know, without any doubt, that our sovereign Lord God has everything under control. That in the midst of any craziness, we can breathe easy.

I'll be the first to admit that I don't have this completely figured out yet, but I want to get there. And I believe the key to it, just as with David and sorta like that dark cave, is for you and me to think less about the reality before us and focus more on the reality of who our Sovereign God is.

And if that starts with learning more about our Lord God through his Word, well, we're all starting in the right place.

Dare—Have an opportunity to spend time in a cave? No matter how cheesy, just schedule it, and then do it. Extra points if you have to crawl around or use ropes.

Double Dare—Caving is daring, and so is talking to people you don't know. Next networking function, party, or whatever, find someone who looks nothing like you at all and engage them in conversation. Introduce yourself and ask at least three good questions to chat over. After your three, if they aren't wanting to talk, you're done. Good work.

Triple Dare—Everybody around you, no matter how young, seemingly uneducated, or unlike you, still knows at least one thing you don't, and perhaps never will. Your mission? Engage them in conversation and try to get them to share it.

The Mountaintop

The purpose of spiritual highs
Read Matthew 17:1-8

Y ou have it too, right? The call to push harder, to climb higher, to discover what waits at the top or lies just on the other side?

Time is obsolete when you're pulled toward the unknown, which trades a commitment-filled reality for one that demands only an open heart and a little endurance. You have it, too. It's the essence of an adventurer.

We'd traveled to the edge of Glacier National Park for a wedding. Most of the party contented themselves with hanging out at camp (I'm still not sure what was wrong with them). But to four of us—two guys, two gals—the hiking trails beckoned. We had no doubt we'd return in time for the rehearsal.

We drove to a trailhead and hiked to a towering waterfall. Unclimbable mud and slick moss bordered the right edge of the waterfall, but on the left side, we saw footholds from where we stood. And broad, flat rocks perforated the river—the types of rocks that beg to be used as stepping stones.

The only one of us wearing a watch stared at her wrist, silently calculating. "We have time."

"You don't look sure," one guy said.

"I'm not." She grinned and hopped across the river. The heart of an adventurer also pushes boundaries.

Upon closer inspection, we realized the footholds weren't all user-friendly. One of them required our 6'4" companion to leap, hoist himself up, and then reach down to assist the rest of us. The 5'3" watch-wearer required a boost, but soon (soon-ish) all four of us stood at the top of the waterfall. The water moved swiftly and restlessly over the edge, free falling to the world below. We jumped across more God-provided stepping stones anchored against the current and came to a narrow plateau on the opposite side of the river.

We scooted toward the edge of the cliff but couldn't see down to the bottom. A powerful gust of wind forced me to back up. We weren't on some cushy trail created by the National Park Service, complete with nailed-in railroad ties, fluorescent-orange safety warning signs, and guardrails that would brace against a fall. This was pure nature, unrestrained and uninhibited.

The dizzying distance to the bottom made for a brief viewing.

Two of us dropped to our hands and knees and slithered to the edge on our bellies. The dizzying distance to the bottom made for a brief viewing. Though only my fingertips and head hung over the edge, I felt that at any moment I would slip into oblivion. *Yep. That's enough.* Even shifting onto my knees to crawl backwards, away from the edge, terrified me.

Once a safe distance from the edge, I stood and allowed the view to settle within me. I felt energized and strong, and I wanted to stay in that moment for hours, if not days. Nothing existed beyond God's beautiful creation and the people I was sharing it with. Everything else fell away: stress, fear, insecurity, pride—I felt nothing except joy and the presence of the Holy Spirit up there on a mountaintop.

(And, yes, we did arrive a bit late to the rehearsal, but it was *totally* worth it.)

There is a reason that spiritual highs are nicknamed "mountaintop experiences." During a mountaintop experience, whether a retreat or a mission trip, everyone is passionate about God and what he is doing.

At home, no one seems to be.

Readjusting to our commitment-filled, day-to-day reality is a jerky, unsettling shift. The mountaintop experience is *phenomenal.* Normal life is just so...normal. And everyone else seems so spiritually inferior or unaware.

"There he was transfigured before them. His face shown like the sun, and his clothes became as white as the light. Just then there appeared before them Moses and Elijah, talking with Jesus. Peter said to Jesus, 'Lord, it is good for us to be here. If you wish, I will put up three shelters—one for you, one for Moses and one for Elijah'" (Matt. 17:2-4).

Peter did not want to leave. And why would he? On the mountaintop, he experienced something astounding while in the company of his closest friends. The symbols of the Law and the Prophets held hands with the fulfillment of both.

Normal life consisted of picking up breadcrumbs, arguing with arrogant Pharisees, and cleaning out smelly fishing boats. And Peter didn't know this at the time, but a demon-possessed child waited for them at the bottom of the mountain.

If they remained there on the mountaintop, they could bypass all sorts of stress. Why did they have to descend? Because Jesus did. He understood the mountaintop's purpose—a haven of respite and encouragement. Jesus understood his own purpose, too. And he needed to descend the mountain to fulfill that purpose. The cross waited for him at the bottom.

Isn't it amazing that despite what lies ahead for Jesus, his next words to Peter are, "Get up. Don't be afraid" (Matt. 17:7).

Like Peter, I wanted to stay. I encountered a peace that passes understanding and I didn't want to walk away from it. But we can't be a light to the world if we segregate ourselves from it. Jesus certainly didn't.

Instead, we need to translate the blessings we receive at the top into a message of compassion that those around us in our everyday lives can understand.

Remember, "Get up. Don't be afraid."

Dare—Recall your last mountaintop experience and think about, or journal, what the experience meant to you then. Review any notes or photos. How have you applied that experience since returning?

Double Dare—Recall your last mountaintop experience that came as a direct result of your church leaders. Catch your pastor, men's group leader, Bible study facilitator, etc.… and tell them you appreciate all they do and that it's having an impact.

Triple Dare—Go find a mountaintop—either literal or spiritual—and allow God to rejuvenate you.

Sat Phone— Listening for God

ver gotten to use a satellite phone? Unless you're in the military, a member of the CIA, or routinely travel internationally in impoverished countries, I'm guessing that, like me, not so much.

Fortunately, it's standard procedure to have a sat phone on wilderness river trips. You have your food, your safety gear, and someone gets the job of leasing, and then carrying, a hard plastic case with the phone.

Sometimes this can be kind of a fun thing.

I remember one trip in which our phone allowed for 60 minutes' worth of free calls. Sweet. My companions' wives had been updated on our progress regularly throughout the month-long trip, with enough time remaining for each of us to make a six-minute call on Christmas morning. When my turn came, I strolled out to the sandy edge of the Colorado River at Granite Park Camp, Mile 209—at the very bottom of the Grand Canyon —and dialed my mom in Bedford, Michigan.

According to her? Best. Christmas Gift. Ever.

But there can be a bit of a learning curve with sat phones. Usually, they're reserved for an actual emergency, when you need to contact someone immediately…and, naturally, absolutely nothing seems to happen.

Yelling is ineffective (feel free), and the sat phone is too costly to hurl at a rock, but each member of the team *will* advance a diagnosis: How's the battery? Fine. Did you try the other antenna? Yup, all good. You're too low, climb higher up the ridge… You get the picture.

After climbing many a steep, rocky ridgeline over the years, with little or no luck finding a signal, please allow me to offer the following hard-won wisdom about successfully putting a call through using your satellite phone, especially in tricky canyon environments.

Sometimes you just have to turn it on, punch in the number, and then…sit there and relax.

That's right. No matter how narrow the canyon, you can always see at least some of the sky, and those leafy cottonwoods aren't blocking your signal either. Even better, you don't have to risk life and limb climbing up some sketchy canyon wall. Nope, just sit patiently and watch as the signal indicator starts to light up and slowly grows in strength. Eventually it will top out at five bars, even though you've been sitting motionless on your log.

Looking up, you can almost see the satellite passing in a wide arc high over your head. You sit still, it comes to you, and then, as it slowly passes out of your line of sight, you lose the signal again.

Simple, and no dangerous, exhausting climbing required. Silly me...

The spiritual parallel of waiting on God is pretty obvious. We want so badly sometimes to find, hear, and see him, yet nothing seems to be happening. And so we spend a great deal of time and effort furiously trying to change our viewpoint, eliminate barriers, and do whatever it takes to be more aware of our Heavenly Father.

Except sometimes we're really bad at remembering to just sit quietly and wait for God to speak.

Certainly there are things we can do to improve our receptivity towards God. Spending time in his Word, in solitude, or out in nature are frequent answers to the question of how to better hear him. I knew a guy that needed only to sit and listen to praise and worship music for a few minutes to make the busy world fade away, leaving him perfectly tuned to God's voice.

What is it you do to hear God more clearly? Give up media? Skip meals? Exchange TV time for prayer time? Whatever it is, good for you. We can't aim higher than doing things that align our hearts and minds with our Creator's voice, but then, of course, once we're there, let's not forget to give him time to speak.

———

The Lord said [to Elijah], "Go out and stand on the mountain in the presence of the Lord, for the Lord is about to pass by."
1 Kings 19:11

It's easy for you and me to echo the Prophet Elijah's experience, looking for God in the fire, or we'll seek the Lion of Judah in the raging wind. But let's not forget that, all too often, the Creator of heaven and earth is simply speaking to us in a gentle whisper. One oh so easily drowned out by the chaotic noise of the world around us.

So find that thing you can do to best hear from God. Maybe plan to invest a few hours in it. Put down the paperwork, turn the phone to silent, and...what? Take a drive by yourself? Pop in the earbuds and go for a run or a bike ride?

Whatever it is—enjoy it for all it's worth, and don't forget to take a few minutes right there in the middle to clear your thoughts, pause, and listen for whatever that still, small voice is dying to share with you. In a quiet moment, away from the everyday distractions of life.

Are you listening for God's gentle whisper?

Dare—Can you clearly answer, "What do you do to best hear from God?" Yes? Excellent. Plan to take advantage of it over the next few days to tune in, and then just quietly listen for 10 minutes.

Double Dare—While sitting in silence for 10 minutes, stay purposeful. Every time your mind wanders into schedule, problems, needs, etc., think of three things you're thankful for, then continue.

Triple Dare—Not sure? Time to experiment. Music? Singing? Solitude? Wilderness? Prayer? God's Word? Fasting meals? Fasting media? Pick one, give it a try, and then assess how receptive you are to God. More so? Perfect. If not, try another tomorrow.

Never Chase A Wolf

God is not elusive
Read Genesis 18:1-15

I was sitting at the campfire, reading my Bible, when I had the bone-chilling sensation of someone watching me. I looked up. Fifteen feet away, on the opposite side of the fire, stood a gray wolf—one of the most majestic and formidable creatures I have ever seen. His narrow, black eyes cataloged my every movement.

A friend and I had driven to Crater Lake in Oregon and set up camp on the edge of Diamond Lake. Words do not do this corner of God's creation any justice, so, I'm sorry, but you're going to have to drop what you're doing and book a flight for PDX—Portland, OR.

I always wake up extremely early when I'm camping. Sleep is merely a formality. I knelt in the dirt, in the gray of dawn, and stirred the embers from the night before. Some dry fir needles, a steady breath, and several sticks later, I warmed myself against the chill of the morning with a decent-sized fire.

Oblivious to the predator in the nearby woods, I sank into my camp chair and cracked open my Bible. I never heard him approach, but I caught something in my peripheral. There he was, unmoving, where the edge of the campsite backed up into the woods. The line between his world and mine.

Cold dread burned through my system. *Weapon.* My gaze darted from the burning logs in the fire pit to the rock beside my chair.

Camera. No one would believe me. I slowly reached down to my left, only to realize my camera was in the minivan, doubling as our tent.

I silently begged the wolf not to move, but it was, after all, a wolf. I carefully stepped toward the minivan. The rumble of the sliding-door spooked the skittish creature and he retreated into the woods. For reasons I cannot explain, I chased him into the trees.

Rule #491 of Survival: Never chase a wolf.

The sun was rising, but the forest was still dark, and I didn't have my flashlight. Only when I registered these facts did my "think-this-through"

139

kick in and I realized the futility—and stupidity—of pursuing a wolf through the wild. Looking around me, disappointment over not getting a picture quickly turned to concern. I couldn't see the wolf, but he very likely could still see me.

Fully aware that this is how so many horror movies begin, I slowly backed away in the direction of the campfire. I'd just as soon a 180-pound predator not eat me for breakfast.

Do you ever feel like God is elusive? Like he is some majestic, out-of-reach being who is content to watch you from a distance? And the moments in which you feel as if you might have encountered him are so fleeting that it is difficult for you to believe it happened, much for less anyone else?

"I will surely return to you about this time next year, and Sarah your wife will have a son" (Gen. 18:10).

Abraham was 99 years old and told by God that he and Sarah would have a child. I recently saw something in the text that I'd never latched onto before. "I will return around this time next year."

Abraham encountered God, literally walked beside him. In my mind, that is a fairly noteworthy event.

Good thing it's noted in Genesis 18.

But don't you think it would also be worthy of notation if God stopped by your home to cradle your newborn child? Isaac's birth, in Genesis 21:1-7, doesn't mention God's house call. It's like trying to read a story with several pages ripped out, and to be honest, I feel a little gypped. But because God promised he would be there around the time Isaac was born, we know that God showed up.

There was nothing skittish about Christ's journey to the cross.

And God is here. Emmanuel—God with us (Matt. 1:23). *"And surely I am with you always, to the very end of the age"* (Matt. 28:20). God crossed the line between our camps the day he manifested himself in the infant Emmanuel. At any point, he could have said, "Forget them, they aren't worth saving," and bolted. But, there was nothing skittish about Christ's journey to the cross.

He came for us and he stayed for us.

You will seek me and you will find me when you seek with your whole heart.
Jeremiah 29:13

God promises that he'll be here, so he is. Our perfect fellowship with God, which was destroyed in the garden, was restored with the cross, which means we can talk to God whenever we want. If you imagined God in the room with you right now, where would he be sitting? What would you say to him?

Even though God has never sat beside me at a campfire *the way he did with Abraham,* I've still met God beside a campfire.

And no matter what your circumstances, God meets you where you are. Seek him. Find him. Acknowledge his presence in your life.

Dare—When is a time in your life when you recognized God's presence? If at all possible, bring this question to mind when you're next to a campfire and can continue your thoughts late into the night.

Double Dare—Have an animal rescue sanctuary nearby? Look into visiting sometime soon and seeing some truly magnificent animals, up close. Bring a friend and trade stories of your best wild animal encounters afterwards.

Triple Dog Dare—Book a flight to Portland (or Eugene), Oregon and seek out Crater Lake.

Bad Moments—Fruits of Self-Control

Sometimes good things just spill out
Read Galatians 5:13-23

Working as a commercial rafting guide, you tend to remember those moments when you came close to almost losing a life. Standing on the beach that day, we had just wrapped up one of those moments.

It was in the second half of the season, when the water levels had begun to drop. A fellow guide had taken a bad line in a large, Class IV rapid. As a result, his boat, filled with customers, was now hopelessly tangled in a pile of rocks, just below the surface on river left. As we moved in to free him, a pod of boats from another outfitter came through the rapids, and sure enough, one of their guides got his boat into the very same predicament.

Already in place, we got the okay from the other company's guide to continue our rescue, helping their people out, too.

Taking on the rescuer role, I carefully made my way out from shore and onto the pinned rafts, both bouncing wildly in the current. Keeping my weight on the downstream tubes, hoping the boats would remain upright, I made contact with everyone, and explained the plan. Taking a deep breath, I then held each person's hand as, one at a time, they carefully crawled over me and slid to the guide waiting back on shore.

Everyone was moving safely, and finally, only one customer was left.

Forgetting all earlier instructions, she moved quickly around me, stepping onto an upstream tube which sank out from under her, immediately dropping her into the water. The current sucked her down and underneath the two pinned boats, straight into what we all knew to be a nearly solid barrier of underwater rocks.

Sounds stopped; no one breathed.

Before I could draw my river knife to saw through the boat floor, someone pointed downstream to a red helmet in the water. Miraculously, the woman had somehow been washed clear of the deadly underwater sieve and was floating downstream, dozens of guides ready to throw-bag her to safety.

Only minutes later, we unpinned the boats and were downstream too, standing on a small beach, surrounded by some 40 customers from both groups, all eddied out in rafts alongside one another. Still rattled by the events that had just occurred upstream, we alternated between shaking our heads and laughing with giddy relief.

And so it was, standing on that beach, that I noticed another pod of boats floating past, from the very same company we'd just helped out. The last boat in the group was apparently guided by the trip leader, who was scanning the crowds, and stopped as soon as he saw me.

He started shouting. Really, really loudly.

Which, of course he would, given that we had just saved four of his customers, right? Before I could smile and wave a "You're welcome," he started shouting. Really, really loudly. I wasn't entirely sure what was wrong, but all conversation ceased and everyone looked at him as he slowly floated past. He concluded his rant by pointing a finger straight at me and glaring, a question hanging in the air.

Some 40 heads all pivoted around to look at me, waiting for my response.

Within two nanoseconds my brain reminded me that a) we'd just rescued his trapped customers, b) we'd extricated their pinned boat, yet, c) he was screaming and shouting at us for who even knows what reason, and that d) he's evidently now waiting on an affirmation of some sort from me...?!?

It was time to set things straight. Cue the sounds of a pull-start chainsaw, please...

But then, praise be to our Lord God for wisdom and self-control in that very moment, far beyond what I could ever have asked or even imagined.

That's right, standing there along that crowded riverbank, teeming with guides and customers alike, all stunned into shocked silence and looking at me, I lifted my arm, pointed straight back at him, and called out in a loud, clear voice for everyone to hear, "You got it!"

And that was it. For the second time in less than ten minutes, everyone around me suddenly relaxed and let out a breath they didn't know they were holding.

Boats floated on, groups dispersed, and I looked over at my fellow rescuer, shook my head, and smiled, saying, "You know, I really do love it sometimes when I just shut up."

I wish I could say that adrenaline had dulled my brain that day (it hadn't), or that my heart was perfectly aligned with the endorsement in James 1:26 of "bridling your tongue" (it wasn't). No, the Bible explains my inexplicable actions in that moment only as a direct result of God's presence within me.

"But the fruit of the Spirit is love, joy, peace, forbearance, kindness, goodness, faithfulness, gentleness and self-control" (Gal. 5:22-23).

One voice in us competes for self-indulgence and anything that benefits us, even at others' expense. The other though, God's Holy Spirit, encourages us to reflect Christ and be an example of his teachings.

And apparently, like the concept of muscle memory, responding to the Spirit can become ingrained and almost automatic if you do it often enough. Consider the church in Macedonia, giving generously despite their poverty:

"This was totally spontaneous, entirely their own idea, and caught us completely off guard. What explains it was that they had first given themselves unreservedly to God and to us. The other giving simply flowed out of the purposes of God working in their lives" (2 Cor. 8:5-7 MSG).

Corinthian believers giving cheerfully 2000 years ago, and then me, standing at the bottom of a river gorge, suddenly drawn to choose grace; de-escalating a tense situation instead of following my first instinct to open fire. Amazing. A complete by-product of my walk with Christ, allowing me to respond with a peace and self-control that were so obviously not my own.

We attempt to live a Christ-like life and good things unexpectedly spill out of us. You tell me, is that helpful to have, or what?

———————

See what happens when you create an environment where good things can spill out of *you*.

Dare—Today, unless it's immoral, unethical, illegal, or life-threatening, the answer to anything (pick one) your wife, friend, or co-worker asks you is, "You got it."

Double Dare—For the remainder of this week, unless it's immoral, unethical, illegal, or life-threatening, the answer to anything (pick two) your wife, friend, or co-workers asks you is, "You got it."

Triple Dare—Same Dare as above, except you share this with your wife *first* and warn them to be careful what they ask for. End of the week— How does knowing the answer is always "yes" change the way your wife relates to you?

Triple Dog Dare—Same Dare as above, except you tell them they can also have some fun with it. End of the week—How does knowing the answer is always "yes", and the freedom to have fun, change the way your wife relates to you?

145

It Could Have Been Worse

Allowing God to navigate
Read Isaiah 43:1-7, 14-19

For one week every summer, my family fills up a resort in the northern woods of Wisconsin. As kids, we woke each morning at 7:00 am, eager to squeeze every last drop of fun out of the day. It was during one of those childhood vacations that nearly all of the cousins learned to water ski.

Flares shot into the air, announcing a new skier's attempt. Bullhorn announcements shooed everyone from the space between the raft and docks. Cousins piled into the boat until it overflowed, arguing about whose turn it was to spot. Everyone else filed onto the docks in anticipation.

The engine sputtered and the odor of gasoline wafted through the air. Shouts of encouragement rang out from all those watching. Last-minute instructions from the water-spotter: *heels down, knees bent, legs together.* A quavering *hit it*, from the skier and the boat accelerated, followed by the moment of truth. This process was repeated for hours each day.

Fifteen years later, well…

One morning, my cousin and I were relaxing in camp chairs on the shore. Nearby, in the space between two docks, waves slapped up against a two-foot mound of grass. A rope secured a blue paddle boat to one of the docks. The older cousins were now parents, and their children were swimming between the raft and the dock.

One boat was missing. "Is someone skiing?" my cousin asked. There was disbelief in his voice because, first of all, it was early—10:00—and second, bundled in a hoodie and sweats and dressed like an Eskimo in the middle of July, he obviously had no intention of getting in the water any time soon.

As he spoke, the boat zipped around the perimeter of the lake toward the dock, pulling a skier—Eskimo's younger brother, who happened to let go of the towrope at the precise moment that several kids jumped off the raft and into his path. My breath froze in my lungs.

"Move!" shouted Skier-cousin. His desperate cry launched the kids into a panicked flurry that only made things worse. He had few options. Decapitate the children swimming in the water, or clothesline himself at the knees with the dock. Either way, it seemed a major injury was inevitable.

But Skier chose a third option. Lightning-quick, he threw his weight onto his side and managed to pivot 90 degrees to the right. He careened through a seven-foot gap between the blue paddle boat and the adjacent dock. His ski tips hit the dirt mound at the lake's edge. His feet were jerked out of the boots.

And he stepped right onto land.

"Hey, guys," he said. Dry as a bone, and still in his life jacket, Skier sat down in a chair beside us.

"Good morning," Eskimo and I replied. Three casual seconds passed before we burst into a frenzy of conversation and laughter.

"I thought I was a goner," he confessed.

A decade later, the perfection of that moment still astounds me. His speed and size could have landed one of the children in the hospital with a head injury. The dock could have broken his legs. Yet, my cousin walked onto land as if nothing had happened.

How often does life trap us with obstacles that we find overwhelming? And yet, through it all, God begs, "Let me navigate this for you."

Even through the darkest valley of the shadow of death, I will fear no evil for you are with me.
Psalm 23:4

King David acknowledged the enemies that he faced on all sides. The Philistines incessantly attacked from their position on the Mediterranean Sea. Yet, David chose faith over fear. "I will fear no evil for you are with me."

Several generations later, in Isaiah 43:1, 2, the author writes:

"Do not fear...when you pass through the water, I will be with you; and when you pass through the rivers, they will not sweep over you. When you walk through the fire you will not be burned; the flames will not set you ablaze."

When the Assyrian army invaded Israel from the northeast and marched them into exile, the Israelites literally waded through waters— rivers, creeks and streams. And I'm sure they passed through villages set ablaze and charred. Despite these horrors, Isaiah said encouragingly, "God is with you. Do not fear."

And let's not forget the Israelites in Moses' day—the Egyptian army bearing down from one side, an impassable Red Sea on the other. Impassable, that is, until it's not. God says, "I've got this," swipes a finger through the water and presto!

Have you ever felt powerless? Enormous life decisions being made for you, yet you are forced to scramble and problem-solve?

The same God that parted the Red Sea (Ex. 14:21-22) wields the power and desire to manifest paths in your life out of what seem like dead ends. Fear not, for he is with you. Scripture repeats this again and again... and again. The phrase "Do not be afraid/do not fear" is found 87 times in the Bible!

God has had plenty of practice managing difficult situations. Although it's terrifying, when we walk in faith and surrender our steps to God, he will see us through to the other side.

Pray through your obstacles. Seek out friends to pray with you and for you. And then walk in faith, and wait. God is working out the solution, even if you can't see it yourself. You may feel as if life is about to take you out at the kneecaps, but God already has your landing all worked out.

Dare—When was the last time you knew, without a doubt, God saved your bacon? Thank him again, have a laugh, and remind him that you fully trust that the God who saved you once, is more than able to do it again and again.

Double Dare—Write a list of everything currently stressing you out. Walk outside, set the paper on fire and watch it burn. Before it burns you, drop it into water. This is you, trusting God to guide you through water and flame.

Triple Dare—Take a walk today and bring all your worries with you. Mentally throw your worries to either side as you walk, or prayerfully give them to God. When you're fresh out of worries, thank God that you truly can, "Cast all your anxiety on him because he cares for you" (1 Pet. 5:7).

Satan's Suckhole

Once you've floated past, it's past
Read Hebrews 12:1-3

I t's a river feature affectionately called Satan's Suckhole, and we were floating straight towards it. A huge pour-over in the middle of the river, it's known for its large recirculating wave accompanied by a strong upstream current that loves to grab boats floating past.

On this particularly sunny afternoon we were planning to have some fun, deliberately paddling our boat into this current, and letting ourselves be sucked into the waterfall where we'd be tossed around and guaranteed some high adrenaline excitement.

"Be sure to lean into the boat, and pay attention to commands," I told my crew. Too many times I'd put boats into this beloved river feature, only to be immediately washed back out. "We can't stay in long if you don't paddle, so get ready to work hard and let's have some fun!" I called for forward strokes and in we went.

The boat caught the current, spun quickly, and was slowly drawn back upstream, into the churning water. With little warning, the river grabbed the upstream side of the raft and pushed it violently downward, filling it with water. As I called for paddle strokes, my customers screamed with surprise, missed the commands, and we quickly washed out of the "suckhole."

We pulled into shore just downstream, grabbed a rock, and as my crew's laughter quieted, we prepared to watch the other boats from our group take their turns getting flung around.

One by one, boats bounced through, punctuated by their own screams and laughter, until finally the last boat started in. This time, however, the crew continued to paddle, and despite the boat being violently tossed repeatedly by the wave, they managed to keep themselves in the hole.

With all boats watching from downstream, they spun, twirled, and bounced around, the boat filled with water, all eyes wide, and their guide calling out rapid-fire paddle commands: "Back hard! Stop! Now forward hard! Keep going!"

My crew looked on in giddy, paddle-clenching awe until the boat eventually flushed out. Immediately one of my paddlers asked the question I knew was coming, "So why didn't we stay in there as long as they did?"

Gently, I reiterated the pre-rapid instructions. "Remember, you have to keep paddling or you get pushed out. When we dropped in, everyone screamed and stopped paddling, so we washed out right away. If you paddle hard though, like that last boat, you can stay in longer and have some really crazy fun!"

"So can we go back up and do it again?"

Everyone made disappointed noises, but nodded with understanding. One girl paused and asked the most logical question possible in light of this information, "So can we go back up and do it again?"

Ah, if only.

The Bible addresses this feeling in Ephesians when Paul encourages us to live our lives, "...making the most of every opportunity, because the days are evil" (Eph. 5:16).

Regret pervades our everyday lives whenever we catch ourselves thinking, just like that young girl, "I wish I could go back and do *that* one over again." The split-second decision I missed. That situation where I could have performed so much better than I did. Those once-in-a-lifetime moments when you could have chosen differently, been more engaged, or simply selected a path you knew to be better.

But instead, for whatever reason, when the moment of truth came you lost your focus and immediately "washed back out." Found yourself "downstream," regretting your missed opportunity, and desperately wanting another chance.

Luckily, the Bible also addresses this yearning in us, with proven advice from Jesus himself, to avoid lingering on past regrets. Jesus tells us, "No one who puts a hand to the plow and looks back is fit for service in the kingdom of God" (Luke 9:62).

Sure there are valuable lessons in our rearview mirrors, but we are instructed to glance at them, not fixate. Assess the poor choices, note the lessons learned, and then move on, ready to apply those lessons in the inevitable obstacles you'll encounter "downstream."

... run with perseverance the race marked out for us.
Hebrews 12:1

Whether birthdays, New Year's, or any other annual opportunity for reflection, we have to ask ourselves, "Am I too attached to something that happened in the last year? A failure I can't let go of? Maybe a missed opportunity that still haunts me?" Whatever it is, we're cheerfully encouraged not to worry, "Do not be anxious about anything" (Phil. 4:6), but to let go, "...let us throw off everything that hinders and the sin that so easily entangles" (Heb. 12:1), and continue down the path God has for us, eagerly ready to use whatever we've learned along the way, "...let us run with perseverance the race marked out for us" (Heb. 12:1).

As our boat prepared to push back into the current and continue on downstream, I told my crew that there was another surf wave down around the next bend. "It's pretty tricky," I cautioned them, "but if you paddle hard and listen really close, we just might be able to catch it." All eyes were on me. "So, does anyone want to try?"

Everyone broke into smiles and a resounding, "Yes!" filled the boat.

And so with paddles in hand, eyes wide with expectation and everyone listening attentively, we paddled off, ready to put our experiences into practice and catch another wave, waiting for us just downstream.

Dare—Ask anyone and they'd rather hear stories about fails and embarrassing blunders than the boring day-to-day. Try to conceive for yourself, if only in your own mind, any humorous elements of your past failures.

Double Dare—Have some big regrets? Don't we all? Ask yourself what can be learned through those past mistakes, and then give them to God. For good. Now that they're forgiven, treat those regrets the same as you would any lustful thoughts or revenge fantasies trying to sneak into your mind from now on.

Triple Dare—Let someone share a regret that *they* see you struggling with. You choose—a trusted friend, your wife, or maybe even one of your kids. Would you have thought of this? Why would they? Consider re-visiting the Double Dare with this information...

153

Don't Trust Satan

Embracing love when it's awkward
Read John 13:1-15

I can still feel the scream in my throat, the bottomless feeling in my gut, when I saw my grandfather emerging from the woods.

I'd gone horseback riding with my grandpa in Wisconsin one summer. When the ranch hands introduced us to the sleek, purple-black 16-hand horse he'd be riding, we laughed. But Grandpa still climbed up on Satan's back.

It was so bizarre to see him astride a horse. We usually spent time together in clean, air-conditioned restaurants that played classical music behind the din of polite conversation. Now he was outdoors, on a smelly animal, in the sticky summer heat, with all manner of annoying insects buzzing around him. Not his element. By a long shot.

My grandpa, a gruff World War II veteran, spoke little and was not given to displays of affection. Intimidated by his hard exterior, I usually kept my distance. But horses were my thing, not his, and as I saw how rigidly he sat in his saddle, I couldn't help but realize this outing was evidence of his love for me.

At the end of the ride, we trotted out of the woods toward the barn. That is, I thought we had. When I turned around, I didn't see Satan. Even after I dismounted, I saw no sign of him—or his rider.

We heard Satan's thundering hooves before we saw them. Horse and rider burst into the clearing at a gallop—Satan running with a slipped shoe. For a man who didn't ride, it was incredible that Grandpa somehow managed to keep his seat. Suddenly the saddle's cinch loosened and it listed to one side. Next it slipped entirely, sliding practically beneath the horse's belly. My grandpa grabbed the reins, attempting to stay on. Satan's head jerked hard to the left and he reared, pawing furiously at the air.

The old man slipped from the saddle, but his right foot caught in the stirrup.

"Grandpaaaaaaaaaa!" The cry tore from my throat, so foreign to me that I actually startled myself. A jolt of adrenaline shot through my body like lightning and I clutched my arms around the void in my gut, watching helplessly.

Ranch hands grappled for the loose reins and fought to subdue Satan. They wrangled his front hooves back down to earth. While they freed my grandpa's foot from the stirrup and escorted him away from the horse, Satan stomped at the ground. His red nostrils flared with exertion.

I wrapped my arms around his middle with abandon. His whole body stiffened.

Miraculously, my grandpa remained uninjured. The foot that caught in the stirrup saved him from being trampled by the horse. I raced toward him and wrapped my arms around his middle with abandon. His whole body stiffened. Only then did I realize my display of intimacy. But I didn't let go. Not right away.

In John 13, the author describes Jesus washing his followers' feet. "The evening meal was in progress, and the devil had already prompted Judas, the son of Simon Iscariot, to betray Jesus. Jesus knew that the father had put all things under his power, and that he had come from God and was returning to God; so he got up from the meal, took off his outer clothing, and wrapped a towel around his waist. After that, he poured water into a basin and began to wash his disciples' feet, drying them with the towel that was wrapped around him" (John 13:2-5).

The encounter between Jesus and Judas passed without incident to the casual observer. Yet, just a few hours later Jews and Romans arrested Jesus and stripped him. They robed him as a mockery, and then stripped him again, not only of his clothes, but also of his dignity, his life. And the catalyst was Judas, Jesus' friend. Jesus withstood Satan's temptation (Matt. 4:1-11), only to be taken down because Judas succumbed to it (for a modern-day equivalent of $3K).

Awkward to love the man whose actions will lead to your death? Definitely. The devil had already prompted Judas (John 13:2). But Jesus, even knowing Judas would betray him, knowing what would happen next, removed his garments—his position—willingly, in the presence of his disciples. And, in case the disciples didn't understand the gesture, he knelt at their feet. And just in case of any lingering confusion, he touched and washed the dirtiest part of their bodies. Peter got it. It horrified him.

The only way for Jesus to wash away our sin was to allow our filth to cover him.

True love embraces the awkward. My grandpa lived in a suburb of Chicago, surrounded by concrete for miles. His comfort zone did not include horseback riding. Yet, comfort took second place to love.

I will not go so far as to say earth was outside Jesus' comfort zone, but it certainly wasn't God's normal stomping grounds.

Unlike my grandpa, God knew what he was walking into. Awkward beliefs. Awkward sin. Awkward people. That's why he walked into it. He embraced the unloved and the unlovely throughout his time on earth. And in the end, he did not withhold his love from the one who would turn against him, but instead loved him as completely as he did everyone else.

True love embraces awkward.

Jesus often calls us to step beyond social convention, to embrace the awkward in order to display love to someone else. He loves us with the same abandon.

So, on to "awkward love" dares. (It wouldn't be too far from the truth to imagine me rubbing my hands together with anticipation.)

Dare—Tell a buddy that you're grateful for him because...? Generosity, kindness... be specific. (Tell him your devo book made you do it.)

Double Dare—Grab any female in your life—wife, daughter, etc.—and dance with her in full view of everyone else. (Awkward, sure, but in 20 years, just ask your little girl if she still remembers it.) And no excuses for weather.

Triple Dare—Any awkward relationships coming to mind while reading this devo? Who is the last person on earth who'd expect you to wash their feet? Make the first move. Shoot them an email to say you appreciate something about them.

Triple Dog Dare—Call the person above and ask if he/she has any prayer requests. Tell this person you're praying for them.

A Plague

Functioning as the body of Christ
Read 1 Corinthians 12:18-20

A mixed company of eight. In four canoes, following a river. During a scorching July. Guys in swim trunks, girls in swimsuits and shorts, and not much else.

We unclipped our life jackets, sliding up to an island campsite. At first, the small clearing seemed a perfect, tranquil place to set up camp. We laughed and joked as we secured the canoes on shore and removed the gear. We leisurely discussed where to set up camp, nonchalantly swatting a mosquito or two.

Then, out of nowhere, they swarmed: a thick cloud of mosquitoes dropping down among us like a plague. We swatted at our vulnerable arms, legs, backs, stomachs, faces—a veritable mosquito feast. Girls shrieked, guys yelled, helpless for only a moment. Then, action.

I have no recollection of conversation, instruction or direction, only of movement. And, movement so swift and efficient, that it will take you longer to read about it than it took for the event itself to occur.

Two people grabbed one tent, two people another. The poles clicked into place. The tent bags were unrolled. Two others grabbed a fire-starter and a lighter. One got the smoke and flame going while the other dashed around the small clearing, gathering kindling and firewood. The remaining two people sprinted to the canoes, grabbed and twisted our soggy towels, and darted from person to person, whipping mosquitoes off the bare skin of the tent-builders, fire-starters and themselves.

Nylon stretched taut over poles. A huge campfire chased the worst of the mosquito threat away. We pitched bags into the tents and dove in right after, sighing with relief and erupting into belly-aching laughter.

I called to a friend in the other tent. "You want some alcohol wipes* for the bites?"

---

*Some camping uses for the alcohol pads in your medical kit: cleaning your face; bug bites (takes away the itch/sting); antiseptic for cuts; (dried-out) fire-starter.

"Yeah, thanks!" I busted them out and performed the lightning-quick exchange. Inside our shelters, we cleaned the bites and dressed in protective clothing before reemerging, applying bug repellent, and bulking up the fire.

We thoroughly enjoyed the rest of our evening as we ate and laughed around the campfire. But no one mourned when we left early the next morning. In fact, we crawled into the canoes fully dressed over our swim-suits and didn't remove long-sleeved T-shirts or pants until we were on our way down the river.

To this day, I don't think I've ever seen a more impressive example of what teamwork can achieve. We couldn't all start the fire. And snapping towels may not have been the sexiest job—although to be honest, I think those guys had the most fun, given that, how often do you have a truly legitimate excuse to towel-whip your friends?

What I remember the most was the willingness to act cohesively, and the speed and efficiency with which each job was handled. The tasks were accomplished without complaining, debating, or committee-forming. We worked separately, yet together, for the good of everyone in the group.

But in fact God has placed the parts in the body, every one of them, just as he wanted them to be. If they were all one part, where would the body be? As it is, there are many parts but one body.
1 Corinthians 12:18-20

We all need each other. Sometimes we find it difficult to ask for help and can manage it only after swallowing our pride. But your gifts are not the same as the guy's next to you and vice versa. In 1 Corinthians 12, Paul compares the body of Christ to parts of the body, but let's translate:

- Not everyone knows how to fix a vehicle.
- Not everyone can build a shed or rewire an electrical short.
- Not everyone is good at delegation—managing people or organizing details.
- Not everyone can play guitar, design graphic art or draft blueprints
- Not everyone can write a book.
- Not everyone can deadlift 500 pounds.
- Not everyone can teach swift-water rescue in Class IV rapids.

How often do we focus on the gifts and talents that we don't have, rather than developing and using the strengths that we do have? I know I'm guilty. I get jealous of things that my friends can do and *enjoy* doing, while I don't have the first clue.

I promise that others are looking at you and feeling the same way.

Find your "thing" and do it!

Dare—Identify that "thing" that you do. What is it that you accomplish with minimal effort, that you love doing, which you hear yourself saying, "I just," when people ask you to explain it to them? Having trouble putting a finger on it? Ask your "thinker/processor" friends. They'll know.

Double Dare—Translate that into service for others. What can you do with that gift or talent to build up your church, the body of Christ and the world around you? Need help? Ask your "dreamer" friends—the ones who are always coming up with crazy ideas. They will have some answers and one of them will resonate with you.

Triple Dare—Implement any ideas sparked by the Double Dare "within the body." Men's group, church family—join the team. And don't be afraid or embarrassed to ask for help the next time you can't accomplish something solo.

Women and Men

And loving the differences
Read Genesis 2:8-23

A speaker friend and her 20-year-old daughter had flown in from Orlando for a Labor Day weekend in beautiful Glenwood Springs, Colorado. I, too, was invited to join in, and by 9:00 a.m. the following morning, we were all riding our bikes past the trail to Doc Holiday's grave and headed up into the canyon just east of town.

A once-daunting engineering feat that required 10 years to complete in the '90s is now a breathtaking section of the Eisenhower Interstate Highway system which follows the Colorado River through the twisty interior of Glenwood Canyon.

We pedaled along the paved bike path following this magnificent structure, riding briefly next to the speeding traffic, then above it, and finally ducking down under the elevated east/west roadbeds to quietly cycle alongside the shaded riverbank.

The basic physics of this riverside route also meant that we'd ascend for the entire first half, but afterwards would enjoy a pleasant, predominantly downhill glide back into town. Nice.

The heart of our adventure was a short but steep hike up to Hanging Lake, the only hiking trail within Glenwood Canyon and one of the more photographed lakes in Colorado (truly, Google it).

Our granola bars served us well as we scrambled up the "stair-climber" grade to the lake above. By the time we had gawked at the brilliant turquoise waters, descended, and found ourselves riding back towards town again, dinner was firmly fixed in everyone's mind. Crossing the river and dropping back into town, we decided that, rather than stop to satisfy our ravenous appetites by inhaling a pizza, we would return to our friend's house and make a quick dinner there.

Anything involving food sounded fantastic to me.

Which is where we come to the point of the story. Because you see, weakened and bleary-eyed with hunger, I could only sit back eating fistful after fistful of yellow corn tortilla chips and stare in semi-hypoglycemic awe as the gals went about the kitchen, well, doing what gals do in a kitchen.

They complimented the decor. They discussed spice rack options at length. They traded recipes and compared and contrasted 30 different preparation options for corn on the cob. I stood back, quietly chopping vegetables (my job), trying desperately to keep myself from gnawing on a table leg.

Forty-five agonizing minutes later, we sat in the cool, shaded back-yard, eating a lovely green salad, politely tearing into grilled burgers with an array of seasonings, laughing and rehydrating over iced tea. And I stared at them, flabbergasted. Each woman had arrived back at the house just as worn out and starved as I was, yet somehow the circumstance of three women working together in a kitchen worked a kind of magic. They discussed salad fixings, introduced gadgets, and worked through design elements that could be radically improved with a simple, but complete, kitchen renovation.

While I would have happily inhaled a burger back in town and called it done, these ladies turned preparing our meal into an opportunity to share, bond, and connect as if they were old friends. Amazing.

"Haven't you read," [Jesus] replied, "that at the beginning the Creator 'made them male and female'…?"
Matthew 19:4

In this age of equality and gender blurring, it's so easy as men to be lulled into our society's call to over-simplify the difference between the sexes:

- *Beauty vs muscles*
- *High heeled shoes vs pocket knives*
- *Love of shopping vs love of football*

While many women break through convention (my brilliant co-author, for example), it would be ignorant to pretend that God created men and women the same. Our instincts, thought patterns and engineering are different and unique. "Male and female he created them" (Gen. 1:27).

When I hear proponents of "equality" minimizing gender roles or trivializing women's strengths—I can't help but refer back to that kitchen. Women are created with such a natural capacity for connection and caring that us guys can only sit back and stare. Right? Sometimes, it's so easy to get distracted by our differences, though, that we don't pause to appreciate the treasure of who they are.

What amazing gifts have the women in your life enriched you with that you have taken for granted? Is it jumping in with a hug or a kind word when you feel down or hurt? Stopping their agenda to focus on your day when you walk through the door?

These beautiful creatures keep our homes clean, orderly, looking pretty, and smelling wonderful. You might complain about the number of pillows your wife has covering the bed, but would any of us ever really trade eating hot dogs over the kitchen sink for a lovingly made enchilada casserole?

They take care of the kids' extra-curricular activities, doctor appointments and discipline. They make the house a home, dazzle co-workers, and run entire organizations, yet still manage to also be present for us.

For all the talk of women feeling marginalized and unappreciated in our society, maybe we need to take a moment to tell the women in our lives that they astound us, that we are mystified by their accomplishments, and that we so absolutely appreciate them, too.

Dare—Next activity in your life that involves women, be inventive and find something in their uniqueness that you can respectfully compliment (cooking, decorating, fabulous hair…). Extra points if they're over 70 and you can make them blush.

Double Dare—Married? Give your wife the night off. Have flowers and a thank you card on the table waiting for her. When she asks why, *do not* say the devo told me to do it. Instead, say, "To show you that I see what you do, and really appreciate you." Have three specific examples ready to share.

Triple Dare—Married with kids? Give your wife the night off. You watch the kids, take care of dinner, and do the dishes while she's gone. Have the previous Dare's thank you card waiting for her.

Perfect Ticks of Time

Savoring life moments
Read John 21:2-13

A few years back, my husband and I parasailed down in South Padre, Texas. Hanging beneath the rainbow-checkered parachute, my gaze dropped to the world below and then to my husband in the boat. This tick of the clock could not be any more perfect. And then it was. A dolphin pod came into view below me. I saw the white wakes their streamlined bodies created as they crested the surface and dipped down beneath it.

You'll likely catch onto this without my saying so, but most of my perfect life moments have been on the water. Moments in which the sun is glistening across the surface, and as my mind captures the panoramic view, I realize with utter contentment that for this mark of time my life is absolutely, completely fulfilled.

I pray from the bottom of my heart that you have experienced moments in life such as these.

Pre-Jesus of Nazareth, most of the disciples' perfect moments had happened on the water, too—in their weather-worn fishing boats, under the blazing sun.

And then, Jesus.

Moments on water were...different...after Jesus—Peter not drowning, storms calmed, teleportation by boat. There were many breathtaking moments on land, as well. The blind could see, the lame walked, the dead rose to life. There was a crazy moment with a cliff-jumping herd of pigs. And what about the times when Jesus fed thousands of people with just a few loaves of bread?

In John 21, unsure of what they are supposed to do after Jesus' resurrection, the disciples return to what they know and love—fishing.

"Simon Peter, Thomas, Nathanael, the sons of Zebedee, and two other disciples were together. 'I'm going out to fish,' Simon Peter told them, and they said, 'We'll go with you.' So they went out and got into the boat, but that night they caught nothing.

Early in the morning, Jesus stood on the shore, but the disciples did not realize that it was Jesus (John 21:2-4).

Picture the scene. Dawn is breaking. As the sun rises, it casts an ethereal glow onto the crests of the waves. Exhaling, for a brief moment they experience a peace that passes understanding.

Muscle memory makes dragging nets an effortless task for their sun-darkened hands. Their grief has been replaced with joy at the knowledge of Jesus' resurrection. And as each man quietly contemplates the enormous implications of the last three years, they find a silent comfort in simply being together. I often wonder what they were thinking that morning.

They scan the eastern horizon as the sky transforms from deep violet and navy to a dusky blue.

This tick of time could not be any more perfect—until it is.

When you find yourself immersed in a perfect moment, pause, savor, reflect and know that this tick of time is a gift to you from your Creator. Just because he loves you.

They spin toward the shore as a voice calls from the west. "Friends, haven't you caught any fish!" They are slightly confused until the voice says, "Throw your nets on the *other* side of the boat."

Then they laugh. They obey, and know their obedience will be rewarded—because the man on the shore is their friend, Jesus.

It reminds them of the first time that this man called to them from shore, three short years prior. So much has changed since then. They drag in their nets, tearing from the weight of 153 fish.

Peter excitedly jumps into the water. After three years, this surprises none of his friends. 153 fish, a miracle just for the disciples—not because they didn't believe, or that they needed proof, but simply because Jesus wanted to make his friends smile. It was a prayer wink.

Also, maybe he was hungry.

The moment becomes sweeter still when they sit down to share breakfast with Jesus. (Meanwhile, Peter is laying his clothes out on a nearby boulder to dry.)

Recognize the miracles in your own life. And when you find yourself immersed in a perfect moment, pause, savor, reflect and know that this tick of time is a gift to you from your Creator. Just because he loves you.

Dare—Ever wanted to go parasailing? Put it on the calendar, preferably where there are dolphins, too.

Double Dare—Go out with a friend or wife for fish/seafood. Fish tacos, clam chowder, sea bass, your choice. Either tip 30% on the meal, or stop and pray over it…with everyone at the table.

Triple Dare—From now on, tip 25% anytime any waitstaff can see you praying over your meal.

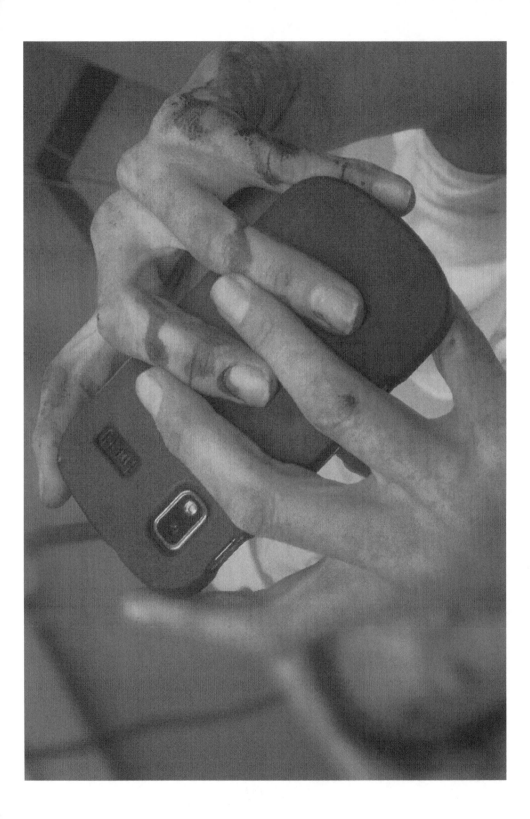

Seeing the Wound— The Devo Experiment

Does God's Word really impact my life?
Read James 1:19-25

There's a fun trick when you're out in the wilderness and someone's hurt and bleeding. And not just bleeding, but bleeding from a spot they can't see. Like their face.

Reflect for a second on the last time you cut yourself shaving and you'll remember one of the basic rules of our circulatory system—nothing bleeds quite like the head. Checking the damage in a steamy bathroom mirror is one thing; seeing blood dribbling down your chin in the wilderness is something totally, unsettlingly, else.

The key to this trick is to simply allow the "victim" to see himself and realize that the wound isn't nearly as bad as they're imagining in their mind. There's a lot of blood for the first minute, but it's all coming from a tiny little scrape on the forehead. Nobody's head has come off, though judging from the bloodbath it can often seem that way.

But how do you allow someone to see himself when you don't have a mirror? Mirrored sunglasses, you say? Sure, but any old sunglasses give a nice reflection if you hold your hand behind them, just like a car window with a dark background. Even better, the glass screen on your cell phone. Cell phone, did you say? Because here's the trick—take a photo of the person—camera, cell phone with no service, selfie, whatever you have—and then hand it to him.

He (or she) will cringe at first, sometimes squeal, then look closer, grimacing more as he starts to connect the blood trail down his cheek with the wound in his scalp. Slowly acceptance will come, and he will hand your camera back, satisfied that he is not dying.

The one thing nobody ever does, ever, when handed a photo of his wounded self? Glance, shrug, and hand it back. Never happens.

Some assess the damage more quickly than others, but rest assured every person will look intently at his appearance, while you stand there patiently.

James uses a similar metaphor to encourage people to not just read the Bible, but to follow its commands. He compares the casual reader to a man who looks at his reflection and then forgets his appearance as soon as he turns away. Absurd! And yet…is it?

"Anyone who listens to the word but does not do what it says is like someone who looks at his face in a mirror and, after looking at himself, goes away and immediately forgets what he looks like" (James 1:23-24).

If I perceive that I am wounded, the best thing you can do is give me a way to ascertain the full scope of the damage. Allow me to examine my appearance and assess where I am flawed so I can understand it or even begin to repair it. Worst case, this self-reflection will at least bring me a peace in knowing the exact extent of my wounds. No more, no less.

So do I approach God's Word believing that I'm flawed, damaged, wounded, and that only his Word can help me understand my injury and ultimately heal me? Or is it just a nice set of rules and checklists? Pleasant ideas for living a friendly life. Maybe it's truly God's inspired Word, but I just can't seem to get into it.

How do you approach God's Word?

I totally understand. The question, though, is if you definitively knew that spending time in God's Word would absolutely have a positive impact in your life, would you look at it more closely? Would you intentionally spend more time throughout the day bringing to mind what you read and pondering the implications?

Have a look at the outline below and consider giving it a try. Here's the plan. Simple as can be, we're going to commit to it for two weeks. Find a good timeframe when you're not traveling or being pulled outside your daily schedule, and commit to the following:

- Read one chapter in the Bible on Monday, Wednesday, and Friday, before you start your day. This devotional is a handy guide for some great chapters to dive into.
- No clue what to read? Here are some recommendations: Romans 12, Philippians 4, Isaiah 40, Ephesians 5, 1 Corinthians 13, and finally Galatians 5.
- Before reading, ask God to show you something in the passage that he wants you to know, do, or understand.
- Ponder what stood out to you in the passage. Is it something good to apply? Something bad to stop? A new way to think of God? An encouraging thought or supportive idea you can share? A new idea to put into practice?

- Write that point or phrase down for later reference. Smartphone reminder, email, notebook, or back of a junk mail envelope. Whatever.
- Come back and ponder this point at every mealtime, and again just before you go to sleep. You just read it, so breakfast should be an easy first step.
- Next day, feel free to ponder the current concept for an additional day.
- On the last day of the two weeks, think through these points:
  - Was I more mindful of God throughout my day during the last two weeks? Did this make a difference for good in my attitude? My words? My actions?
  - Was I more relaxed, confident, peaceful, happy, patient, purposeful, or mindful of others over myself?
  - As a result of being in God's Word, did I notice that I could hear him more readily? His guidance and direction during my day? His encouragement? His support?

Was your life any better for spending time in God's Word and pondering what you read?

Did you notice some real, specific, measurable changes in your attitude or behavior? Being patient with people got a little easier? You were less frustrated in traffic? Maybe you yelled at other drivers, just like before, but it was less satisfying and you did it less, or even stopped?

Take a sober assessment of yourself—your bloodied face, your need for God's Word and the impact it can have on your attitude and behavior —and then join me and thousands of other men tomorrow morning. Let's all have a laugh, make a plan, and take away something from what we are reading in his Word.

Applying it in our lives and changing the way we live. Forever.

———————

Dare—As listed above, read three chapters, three days per week, asking God to show you something you can implement in your life. Evaluate the results at the end of two weeks.

Double Dare—As listed above, read three chapters, three days per week, asking God to show you something you can implement in your life. Ponder each day's point, along with all previous points, as you continue. Evaluate the results at the end of two weeks.

Triple Dare—As listed above, read three chapters, three days per week, asking God to show you something you can implement in your life. Evaluate the results at the end of two weeks with your wife, a trusted friend, one of your kids, or even a trusted co-worker. Ask if they noticed a difference in you.

Devotion 40
—A Final Word

One last adventure together. . .
Read Psalm 40:1-10

Sam:

We walked along a dried-up river bank in late autumn—half a dozen friends and myself. Our boots crunched over hard earth and frost-covered leaves. Despite the frozen ground, my friends minded their footing as they crossed the river bank.

I didn't. I did not leap across the middle as they had done. I feared that I would fall and end up smeared with mud from head to toe, and they, of course, would all turn and laugh at me.

I would safely step across then. Except the frozen river, well, wasn't. My first step stuck a bit, like tack paper. No biggie. On the next step, my boot sunk in about an inch. Annoying to clean, but whatever, I could deal. Then, third step—straight down until ice-cold mud imprisoned my leg from the knee down. There was no way to pull myself out without sinking in deeper.

Eric:

We were on a float trip through Cataract Canyon, the 90-mile section of the Colorado River running from Moab, Utah, down to Lake Powell. Essentially floating through Canyonlands National Park, we came to our camp and decided to hike a nearby side canyon. The sun was blazing and we thought the narrow canyon might provide some shade. Not really.

After hiking through tumbleweed stickers, goat-head thorns, and assorted other pokey stuff, we eventually came to a large pile of branches and debris. Foolishly, I opted to just go around by stepping out into the narrow rivulet of a muddy stream running along the canyon bottom. I lasted three steps before sinking up to my thigh…

Sam:

"Um, guys?" They walked well ahead of me now. At the sound of my voice, they turned, saw me buried in mud and burst into laughter. *Awesome.*

All but one of them remained safe on the opposite shore. Chris rolled his eyes at me, but tromped back. With stable footing, he clamped his hand around my upper arm and pulled me out. He then performed a second rescue operation for my boot.

I lay exhausted on the ground, legs caked in smelly, cold mud, and a yucca bush sticking me in the back.

Eric:

Over my two companions' laughter, I was at least thankful that I'd thought to take off my hiking sandals before straying into the mud. One embarrassing photo and several minutes later, I lay exhausted on the ground, legs caked in smelly, cold mud, and a yucca bush sticking me in the back. We decided to continue on, hoping to investigate the sound of trickling water around the next bend. Anything to wash off the smelly skid marks covering my lower half. They'd helped pull me out, sure, but my friends now politely asked if I wouldn't mind hiking in the back.

Sam:

"I waited patiently for the Lord; he turned to me and heard my cry. He lifted me out of the slimy pit, out of the mud and mire; he set my feet on a rock and gave me a firm place to stand. He put a new song in my mouth, and a hymn of praise to our God. Many will see and fear the Lord and put their trust in him" (Psalm 40:1-3). U2 also turned Psalm 40 into a song—just sayin'.

Some versions say, "He inclined and heard my cry." But you get the idea. You get stuck, God hears you calling out for help and he tromps back through the muck to pull you free. This, friends, is the gospel in one slimy nutshell.

The question is, what did God save you from, and what are you going to do about it?

Eric:

The canyon narrowed and we followed a long sweeping curve, finally seeing the source of the splashing noises. Standing there in the 100-degree heat, our jaws hanging open, we could hardly believe our eyes. A pool of blue water, surrounded by terraced, sandstone rock benches that wrapped gently upwards and around both sides, joining again at the far end, where a waterfall softly splashed. The spell broke and we barely took the time to drop our cameras and water bottles before plunging in.

In a matter of seconds, dry, scorching, desert air morphed into refreshing, cool, clear water. Dust washed away, mud smears disappeared, and we splashed, laughed, and took turns jumping from the rock ledges above.

Many read this psalm as one of salvation, and even restoration (God gave me a firm place to stand), but don't miss the very ending too…joy! Our gracious Lord God removes our hopelessness and shame, and ultimately gives us a "hymn of praise" to sing. We go from being covered in sticky, smelly mud to doing silly backflips into a natural pool, a treasure hidden away in a remote desert canyon. That calls for a hymn of praise, indeed!

Sam:

Joy? Most definitely. I don't remember every weekend of my life, but I will never forget that one. My most vivid image is the laughter in Chris's expression. *You're ridiculous* mixed with *you're fun.* I sometimes wonder if that's how God looks at us…

Devotion 40 is in loving memory of Pvt. Christopher A. Sisson (1983-2003)

O ut of the mire. Joy in the journey. So now what? You've read forty challenging, potentially life-changing devotions. You're on the verge of Adventure Devo graduation. So now what, indeed?

Take a deep breath. It's time for one last dare…

Dare—Share this book, and something you learned from it, with a friend.

Double Dare—Share this book, and something you've learned from it, with a friend and with the person who gave it to you.

Triple Dare—Share this book, and something God is implementing in your life (new habit, new passion, new line in the sand…) as a result of reading it, with a friend and with the person who gave it to you.

Triple Dog Dare—Do the Triple Dare…*and* share it with the community of other guys who have wrestled with, been challenged by, and (just like you) snickered over everything you've read here, at www.AdventureDevos.com.

Afterword

entlemen, the adventure is just beginning. Stay safe, stay well, and go do some amazingness in this world, according to your calling, and to the praise of our glorious God.

Blessings.

Eric Sprinkle and Sam Evans, Winter 2018

About the Authors

Sam "Samantha" Evans

Neatly trimmed nails are nothing a gritty rock face can't fix, and the contents for any five-day trip worth taking can always fit into a single rucksack. Sam believes in the value of perspective. Whether that's the ocean floor, free-falling from 13,000 feet, or staring at a wolf through a campfire, there are life lessons and spiritual applications to be learned. After all, the greatest adventure to be lived is in walking in stride with Christ.

Sam earned degrees from Northwestern University in youth ministry and biblical studies and has been active in various ministry leadership roles for the last eighteen years. Her passion is to challenge Christians to deepen their faith, speaking truth with transparency, humor and love. An unconventional pastor's wife and mother of three, should you dare her to jump into an ice cold lake during wintertime, just remember to bring a towel.

You can connect with Evans at http://lovesamevans.com, on Twitter at @LoveSamEvans, or on her Facebook group, Love Sam Evans.

Eric Sprinkle

Eric is an avid adventurer—having travelled the world, hiking waterfalls in Croatia, swimming with sea turtles in Guam, and scaling active volcanoes in New Zealand—and has seen adventure's impact on people firsthand, over and over again. Founder of Adventure Experience and member of the National Speaker Association, he now travels the U.S. with his award-winning photos, speaking on the benefits of risk, challenge, and getting outside your "comfort zone." He also spends way too much time on local rivers and mountains and has finally given up trying to get the smell of wet neoprene out of his car.

More info at AdventureExperience.net.

Summer Camp *never ends when* your devotional takes you adventuring all year long!

Adventure Devos: Youth Edition

Coming to you Spring 2019

Bring the Adventure to you, at AdventureExperience.net

Need an exciting Speaker at your next Men's Group or work event? Eric speaks on Risk, Challenge, and living life to the fullest – at work, at home, in your relationships, and everywhere in-between.

Connect with him for a variety of thrilling talks, sure to please your group of busy 21st century professionals today!

Come visit us at AdventureDevos.com today!

- Share that **Triple Dog Dare!**
- Sign up for the most beautiful and adventurous newsletter ever.
- Be featured in our emails.
- Leave us your thoughts and ideas on making future Devos more exciting and inspiring than ever before!